## Six Remarkable
# HULL-HOUSE
# WOMEN

# Six Remarkable
# HULL-HOUSE
# WOMEN

### by RUTH BOBICK

Peter E. Randall Publisher
Portsmouth, New Hampshire
2015

ISBN: 978-1-942155-10-2
Library of Congress Control Number: 2015937905

Cover portraits, clockwise from top: Jane Addams, Florence Kelly, Alice Hamilton, Julia Lathrop, Grace Abbott, Edith Abbott Photographs of Addams, Kelly, Hamilton, Lathrop, and Grace Abbott, courtesy of the Library of Congress, Prints and Photographs Division; photograph of Edith Abbott, courtesy of the Research Center, University of Chicago Library

Published by
Peter E. Randall Publisher
Box 4726
Portsmouth, NH 03802

Book design: Grace Peirce

# Contents

# Foreword

*The struggle for social justice of "six remarkable Hull-House women"*
*—Jane Addams, Julia Lathrop, Florence Kelley, Alice Hamilton, and*
*Grace and Edith Abbott—remains little known to this day.*

*The story of their unique contributions, from the Progressive Era*
*to the New Deal, has emerged largely through the efforts*
*of female investigators of the past few decades.*

**It is hoped that the following narrative will lead**
**to further exploration of historical and biographical sources.**

# Introduction, 1893

I n 1893, the fourth year of Jane Addams' Hull-House settlement, two defining events took place in Chicago. The city staged a historic World's Fair to celebrate the four hundredth anniversary of Columbus's discovery of America; and at the instigation of Hull-House reformers, the Illinois legislature passed a landmark factory law regulating work conditions for women and children.

As an industrial, railroad, and commercial center with a population of over a million, Chicago outbid New York in a competition to host the great exposition. From its spectacular opening on May 1, 1893—a year late—to the last day in October when it closed, some twenty-seven million visitors attended, including fourteen million from foreign countries.

Distinguished East Coast architects and the famous landscape designer Frederick Law Olmsted succeeded in transforming over six hundred acres of sand and swamp along Lake Michigan into a spacious park and model "White City" for the fair. Only Chicago architect Louis Sullivan's experimental Transportation Building with its arched golden-doorway departed significantly from the prevailing neo-classicism—which would dominate public buildings in the United States for generations to come. The theme of water was integral to the scene: with the lake, a sculptured "water-gate," large ceremonial basin, lagoon, two ponds, and a network of canals.

Of the ten major exposition buildings, the largest structure— the Manufactures Building—equaled that of four Roman Coliseums. From its rooftop, an observation deck provided a stunning view of the fairgrounds and of Chicago skyscrapers up to seventeen stories high in the distance. At night, a dazzling light show of the imposing "white palaces" and their reflecting-basin with its multi-colored fountains fascinated spectators above all other attractions. As the fair was temporary, the classically-designed buildings were made of "staff"—a mixture of plaster, cement, and jute fibers, with steel or wood frames. For the chief-planner Daniel Burnham, the traditional, imperial architecture created a comforting sense of order and stability, as opposed to the sprawl and turmoil of the industrial city.

Inside the exhibition halls, the latest innovations of science and technology were displayed, as well as a profusion of new merchandise and works of important American artists. Among the exhibits, Edison's Tower of Light, Tesla's alternating current, early "moving pictures," long-distance telephones, and radios with instant transmission testified to American ingenuity and progress, and to the role electricity would play in the twentieth century. Downtown, a series of congresses was featured at the future Art Institute, on such topics as World Religions and Representative Women—the latter with Addams and Julia Ward Howe among its principal speakers. The congress on Settlements was held at Hull-House.

Along the Midway, a mile-long amusement area separate from the White City, an array of ethnic pavilions was situated—including German and Javanese villages, a street in Cairo, Japanese garden, Moorish palace, and Chinese theater. Black musician Scott Joplin introduced ragtime at the Midway, Houdini staged a magic show, and most popular of all, George Ferris presented his revolving steel Ferris Wheel, over 250 feet in diameter. Illuminated at night with some three thousand incandescent lights, it proved to be a breathtaking successor to the Eiffel Tower, icon of the 1889 World's Exposition in Paris.

Meanwhile, in stark contrast to the ideal White City of the fair in its landscaped setting, Hull-House stood in the midst of dilapidated tenements and dirty streets in Chicago's Nineteenth Ward. The previous year, Florence Kelley—a resident and ardent social reformer—had conducted studies of working women and the city's sweatshop system for the Illinois Bureau of Labor Statistics. Striking in her account was the extent to which sweat labor had spread throughout the clothing industry.

As described by Kelley, the tailoring trade was fast becoming de-skilled in order to produce large quantities of ready-to-wear clothes as cheaply as possible, without overhead cost. Increasingly, garment manufacturers contracted "sweaters" as middlemen to distribute pre-cut material for unskilled immigrants to finish in dimly-lit sweatshops or cramped living quarters. Men, women, and children labored long hours—ten to fourteen a day—in dingy tenement rooms where outbreaks of contagious diseases often erupted, infecting the workers and contaminating garments.

Paid by the piece at unsustainable wages and laid off seasonally, workers sank further and further into poverty, with women and children at the lowest end of the wage scale. Discovery of the degrading conditions of the sweating system in Kelley's report led to the state legislature forming a commission of inquiry into labor practices in Illinois, focusing upon the employment of women and children. Kelley presented statistics at the hearings in the capital at Springfield, and personally guided the downstate committee on a tour of tenement sweatshops surrounding Hull-House, exposing them to appalling sights and tales of suffering.

As a result, following her draft recommendations, the state investigative committee proposed a minimum age of fourteen for the employment of children, an eight-hour workday for women, and the regulation of sanitary conditions in tenement manufacturing. According to Addams, in order to pass the bill it was necessary to "appeal to all elements of the community, and a little group of us addressed the open meetings of trades-unions and benefit societies, church organizations and social clubs, literally every evening for three months." At the state capital, prominent Chicago clubwomen active in the anti-sweatshop movement joined Hull-House leaders and labor representatives in a vigorous lobbying campaign.

Finally in June 1893, legislators approved the Illinois Factory and Work Shop Bill advocated by the state's labor commission. That July, progressive Governor John Altgeld named Kelley as Chief

Factory Inspector for Illinois, authorizing her to choose an assistant and ten deputy inspectors. It was the first time a woman had attained a position of such authority and influence in the United States—still twenty-seven years before women secured the right to vote.

## Sources

Addams, Jane. *Twenty Years at Hull-House*. NY: Macmillan Publishing Company, 1938, 201.

Bryan, Mary Lynn McCree, and Allen F. Davis, eds. *100 Years at Hull-House*. Bloomington: Indiana University Press, 1990, 23–35.

Miller, Donald. *City of the Century*. NY: Simon & Schuster, 1996, 488–504.

Goldmark, Josephine. *Impatient Crusader: Florence Kelley's Life Story*. Urbana: University of Illinois Press, 1953, 33–38.

Sinkevitch, Alice, ed. *AIA Guide to Chicago*. NY: Harcourt Brace Company, 1993, 13–14.

Sklar, Kathryn Kish. *Florence Kelley and the Nation's Work*. New Haven: Yale University Press, 1995, 206–218.

# CHAPTER 1

# The Hull-House Settlement

In response to the misery and squalor of the industrial city, the first settlement house, Toynbee Hall, opened in 1884 in the slums of East London. It drew inspiration from social critics like John Ruskin, an Oxford art historian who spoke out against the growing inequality between the classes in England. As a reformer, he deplored how the industrial system had robbed the laborer of his skills and the city of its beauty.

Following Ruskin's suggestion that college graduates in search of a meaningful life spend time living in a slum to help remedy its abuses, Arnold Toynbee—a young Oxford lecturer in economics—paid visits to St. Jude's, "the worst parish in London." Its vicar Samuel Barnett, who became his friend, perceived that Toynbee and other university men like him might bridge the gap between the haves and have-nots of industrial society. Barnett went on to establish a "settlement house," which he named Toynbee Hall in honor of the, by-then, respected economic historian (who died all too early at the age of thirty-one).

As an Anglican minister, Barnett was sensitive to the spiritual dimension of poverty. He strove for a spiritual awakening which would come, he felt, when the poor received the benefits of education and culture that were the right of Oxford and Cambridge students. Toynbee Hall was intended to extend such advantages to laboring men—to give them a chance to view art exhibits, attend extension classes, and have access to clubs, concerts, and libraries. In turn, settlement residents and volunteers would be responding to an inner need to do something of value to alleviate the suffering of those trapped in the slums. Over time, Barnett hoped that Toynbee Hall and its neighbors, by acting together, could bring about such improvements as clean streets, better housing, and parks and playgrounds.

For Jane Addams, who visited the settlement in 1888 after reading about it, what she saw was a revelation to her—the answer to eight difficult years she later called her "snare of preparation." Upon graduation from Rockford College, she'd spent a term at medical school in Philadelphia, withdrawn, undergone back surgery along with a lengthy convalescence, and taken two extended trips to Europe, without finding a course of action to pursue her strong sense of purpose. However in the university settlement of East London, she encountered something new—not charity or missionary work, but communication across class lines and educational and cultural outreach to struggling laborers.

The visit to Toynbee Hall, three years after its founding, changed Addams' life. It strengthened a decision she'd been making to open a settlement herself in a run-down area of Chicago, together with her college classmate Ellen Gates Starr. This decision became a reality in September 1889, when the two friends moved into the old Hull mansion on South Halsted Street in an immigrant neighborhood on the city's southwest side. Besides making use of Addams' own inheritance, they sought the support of well-to-do Chicagoans interested in civic reform. And they attracted young, generally college-educated women as residents and as volunteers.

Hull-House wasn't the first American settlement, nor was Addams the first to follow the example of Toynbee Hall in confronting the overwhelming problems of industrialization. In New York City on the Lower East Side, almost simultaneously with Hull-House's opening its doors, College Settlement was founded by a number of alumnae of eastern women's colleges. It was located in the same district as the initial American settlement—Neighborhood Guild—established in 1886 by a pioneering group of men "settlers." In time, several Protestant denominations adopted the settlement idea as an expression of the Social Gospel.

As American settlements developed and spread—over a hundred existed by 1900 and four hundred in 1910—they differed in significant ways from their English model and from each other. First and foremost, women dominated the American scene, while in England men predominated in what became a training ground for civil servants. Second, American settlements put more emphasis on the social environment than their Toynbee Hall counterparts, who stressed the individual. Further, in America the focus was upon the influx of recent immigrants from southern and eastern Europe, while in the East End of London, settlements centered to a greater degree on native-born English speakers. Moreover most American settlement houses, unlike the English, were non-sectarian, serving mainly Catholic, Orthodox, and Jewish workers.

Above all, it was the first generation of college women in America that joined the settlement movement, to a large extent due to the discouraging situation they faced upon graduation. On the one hand, they had ambitions to utilize their advanced education for the benefit of society; on the other, the options before them were restricted—if unmarried, either teaching or missionary work. Or else they were expected to devote themselves to the "family claim," as Addams referred to a single-woman's service to her family. Professional careers like law, the ministry, government, and higher education were reserved for men. As a result, settlement work seemed a natural choice for young women—an outgrowth of their family and household responsibilities, only in this case expanded to the neighborhood and the city.

Of the leading reformers at Hull-House during the 1890s—Jane Addams, Florence Kelley, and Julia Lathrop—each had spent much of the previous decade searching for a suitable occupation. Educated at three of the limited number of colleges admitting women in the '70s and '80s, Addams received her degree from Rockford College, Lathrop from Vassar, and Kelley from Cornell. Since girlhood, they had been encouraged by their fathers—elected political men—to take an interest in public affairs, which disposed them toward political action during a lifetime of working for social reform. In Illinois, John Addams had been a state senator for eight terms, and William Lathrop served in both the state legislature and in Congress. William Kelley, a Pennsylvanian, was a longtime member of the United States House of Representatives from a working-class district. Abolitionists, Protestant Republicans, and advocates of woman's suffrage, they had all known Lincoln personally and admired him.

According to Addams, "the original Hull-House residents wished the social spirit to be the undercurrent of the settlement's life, whatever direction the stream might take." In two talks she gave on the necessity and value of settlements at a summer conference in Massachusetts in 1892, she put the social spirit into a democratic context. In her words, Hull-House was "an effort to add the social function to democracy," based on the "mutual dependence and reciprocal relation of classes to each other." Addams often referred to what she called a "social democracy," one that would extend democracy beyond individual rights, and carry it into the nation's social fabric. She held that "the good we secure for ourselves is precarious and uncertain, is floating in mid-air, until it is secured for all of us and incorporated into our common life."

For Hull-House, its residents and volunteers, that meant translating their humanitarian ideals into social and educational opportunities for poor, mainly immigrant workers overwhelmed by the hazards of the industrial system. As a means of reducing the barriers between classes, Addams considered education to be primary—to be "the foundation of democracy." The settlement, she maintained, could provide a welcoming and hospitable setting for lectures and clubs, for art exhibits and ethnic gatherings—not as philanthropy but in keeping with "the duties of good citizenship."

──⁸ 3 ⁸──

It did not take long, once Hull-House opened, to determine the most pressing of the neighborhood's problems. At that time the Nineteenth Ward of Chicago included some ten thousand Italians, many German and Irish, newcomer Greeks, and Polish and Russian

Jews. Altogether there were almost fifty thousand inhabitants situated in loosely defined colonies. Further south the Jewish population merged into a huge Bohemian colony so great that Chicago ranked as the third largest Bohemian city in the world. The ward had two hundred and fifty-five saloons in its midst, seven churches, plus a number of small synagogues.

As she described the neighborhood: "The streets are inexpressibly dirty, the number of schools inadequate, factory legislation unenforced, the street-lighting bad, the paving miserable and altogether lacking in the alleys and smaller streets, and the stables defy all laws of sanitation. Hundreds of houses are unconnected with the street sewer." Constructed of wood for the most part and designed for one family, they often sheltered three or four households; and were interspersed with newer, higher brick structures that were equally cramped. Many tenements in the back had no running water inside; and garbage was heaped in boxes secured to the pavement along the streets.

Regarding the settlement building itself—again in Addams' words: "Hull-House is an ample old residence, well built and somewhat ornately decorated after the manner of its time—1856. It has been used for many purposes, and although battered by its vicissitudes, is essentially sound and has responded kindly to repairs and careful furnishing. Its wide hall and open fires always insure it a gracious aspect. It once stood in the suburbs, but the city has steadily grown up around it . . ." Helen Culver, cousin and inheritor of the mansion's original owner Charles Hull, let her have it rent free after a year and gradually turned both it and surrounding property over to the settlement.

Whatever her initial plans, Addams was ready to adapt to changing conditions. Right away, the necessity of a day nursery and kindergarten for the children of women "working out" became apparent. Practical classes like English, American citizenship, and sewing and cooking met immediate needs; while boys' and girls' clubs, German and Italian evenings, and a social science club for working men proved popular undertakings. A co-operative residence for working girls, dispensary for sick neighbors, playground for safe play, and five baths available to all, followed—the last two, "trail-blazers" for Chicago and responsible for the city's supplying additional facilities.

In what was one of the earliest planned literary and artistic activities, a reading group of Italian immigrants was formed to hear George Eliot's *Romola* read each week in Italian, with accompanying slides of Florence. Reproductions of art masterpieces from the two founders' European travel were hung throughout the house, with more "on loan" to students and to schools in the district. The incorporation of art into the public schools, introduced by Starr, became citywide when promoted by the Chicago Women's Club as well. The first new Hull-House building was the Butler Art Gallery (named after its donor), where Starr organized exhibits from the collections of wealthy Chicagoans—sometimes seen by as many as three thousand visitors over a two-week period. In 1893 when the Art Institute on Michigan Boulevard opened, Hull-House discontinued its own art shows and arranged for Sunday excursions downtown.

Night classes at Hull-House were the first experienced in Chicago, taught by college graduates, both women and men, residents and volunteers. Special guest-lecturers over time included such figures as the architect Frank Lloyd Wright and the suffrage leader Susan B. Anthony. College extension courses were also offered, conducted by professors from the University of Chicago. Addams felt that the university extension movement was "best done in settlements outside a university setting." In fact she held settlements to be "a protest against a restricted view of education." And for ten years Hull-House operated a summer school for neighborhood girls on the Rockford College campus, her alma mater—away from Chicago's stifling heat. Later a seventy-six acre "Country Club" overlooking Lake Michigan near Waukegan was presented to the settlement by the generous benefactor Louise de Koven Bowen, making a summer vacation possible for children of all ages, and for many mothers too.

Early on, the Chicago Public Library established a branch reading-room at Hull-House, the only one in the district. The third construction in a Hull-House complex that would eventually reach thirteen, covering a city block, was a dual coffeehouse-gymnasium. On the first floor, it provided nutritious food at low cost and served as a gathering place for the public, while upstairs it featured sports activities for youth. A Children's Building and a Boys' Club for vocational training materialized in a few years, the latter with well-equipped shops for woodworking, metalworking, photography, and printing.

In the arts, Hull-House opened up opportunities for musical instruction and dramatic performance, both by staff and by professionals offering their services—as well as training in drawing, painting, and sculpture. A Music School was begun in 1893, with lessons in violin, voice, piano, and other instruments; an orchestra and boys' band; choruses for adults and children; and regular Sunday afternoon concerts by musicians in the area. The Hull-House Players were pioneers in the little-theater movement, with a range of plays extending from Sophocles, to Shaw, to aspiring young settlement playwrights. For their part, junior players enacted fantasies and mixed groups staged ethnic pageants and festivals. In time, Bowen Hall was built with a seating capacity of seven hundred.

Almost from the beginning, women's trade unions played an integral part in the Hull-House program. Rooms were put at their disposal for meetings; and four unions—those of the bookbinders, shoemakers, shirt-makers, and cloak-makers—met regularly at the settlement, with the latter two organized there. It was Florence Kelley, above all others, who turned the settlement in the direction of reform and influenced Hull-House into taking a forthright position on labor issues.

An enterprise close to Addams' heart was the Labor Museum, inaugurated in 1900, which illustrated the history of surrounding industries and of Hull-House activities—for example, of textiles and bread-making—showing their development from a simple seed to a finished product. The ancient skills of pottery and woodcarving, of weaving and spinning, were taught in the hope of instilling a lost pride in the art of handicrafts nearing extinction. As the accomplishments of many immigrant parents remained unappreciated by their city-bred children, those with a past as artisans were engaged part-time as teachers in the museum, stimulating respect for their European heritage.

Looking back later, Addams found her memory of the first years at Hull-House to be "more or less blurred with fatigue, for we could of course become accustomed only gradually to the unending activity and to the confusion of a house constantly filling and refilling with groups of people. The little children who came to the kindergarten in the morning were followed by the afternoon clubs of older children, and those in turn made way for the educational and social organizations of adolescents and of adults, occupying every room in the house every evening." Residents were diversified, as were volunteers. Hull-House was the first settlement to include both women and men—many of whom had official jobs downtown.

As Hilda Satt, a young Polish-Jewish girl in the neighborhood, wrote of Hull-House in *I Came A Stranger*, singling out Addams as head resident: "Her presence was felt everywhere . . . Whether we were reading Shakespeare, or working in the Labor Museum, or dancing in the dancing class, or listening to a lecture or concert, whenever she appeared, the room became brighter. Every time I saw her the thought came to me that if it had not been for her, I would not be enjoying all these things."

## Sources

Addams, Jane. *The Social Thought of Jane Addams*. Edited by
    Christopher Lasch. Indianapolis: Bobbs-Merrill Company,
    1965, 29–35.

———. *Twenty Years at Hull-House*. NY: Macmillan Publishing
    Company, 1938, 93–151.

Davis, Allen F. *Spearheads for Reform*. NY: Oxford University Press,
    1967. vii–ix, chapters 1–3.

Hammington, Maurice. *The Social Philosophy of Jane Addams*.
    Urbana: University of Illinois Press, 2009. See esp. chapters
    4, 5, 7, 8.

Knight, Louise. *Jane Addams: Spirit in Action.* NY: W.W. Norton, 2010, 65–81.

Polachaeck, Hilda Satt. *I Came a Stranger.* Urbana: University of Illinois Press, 1989, 76.

Ruskin John. *Unto This Last.* Edited by Susan Cunningham. London: M. Dent, 1921. Internet Archive: Open Library: https://openlibrary.org/ (accessed 2010).

Sklar, Kathryn Kish. "Hull-House in the 1890s: A Community of Women Reformers." *Signs*, vol.10, no.4 (Summer 1988), University of Chicago Press, 658–677.

# CHAPTER 2

# Crisis of 1893–1894

A dark shadow was cast upon the Great Columbian Exposition as the Panic of 1893 hit Chicago in the summer and fall of that year. When the fair closed in November and the magnitude of the depression became clear to all, a Chicago journalist wrote: "What a catastrophe! . . . What a human downfall after the magnificence and prodigality of the World's Fair . . ." It was the most severe economic crisis up to that time—a breakdown of the industrial system, which lasted until 1897.

With banks collapsing, one-third of factories shutting their doors, and tens of thousands of fair-workers left jobless, unemployment in Chicago reached a high of forty percent. A smallpox epidemic also struck, sparked by a neglected case at the exposition. The bitterly cold winter that followed intensified the suffering. At City Hall where the homeless took refuge at night, it was reported that "every inch of the stone floor of the corridor was covered with men sleeping on newspapers, their wet shoes serving as pillows." The same scene was repeated elsewhere in the city, in police stations, vacant buildings, and churches.

At Hull-House, all the residents "worked under a sense of desperate need," struggling to respond to the dire poverty that had overwhelmed the neighborhood. Addams—in the vanguard of civic attempts to deal with the crisis—joined with Chicago women's clubs "to organize and fund a shelter and a sewing workshop" for destitute women. She served, also, as a leading member of the Civic Federation in their effort to provide "relief stations, temporary shelters, and street-crew work" for those without jobs. But it wasn't enough. Of all the social misery she encountered, she found nothing "so heartbreaking as unemployment"—or as devastating for the sanity and the self-respect of workers.

Prices and wages had fallen to "rock bottom." Nationally, as many as three million were said to be out of work. Hobo camps sprang up; and Coxey's army of jobless men marched on Washington to appeal for work projects—where its leaders were arrested for trespassing on a Capital lawn. But protests against wage cuts and mass layoffs became louder and more vehement as the months passed—protests and strikes arising from sheer desperation and fear of starvation. A major eruption seemed inevitable; and it occurred in May 1894 at the Pullman Railroad-Car Works, south of Chicago.

The Pullman Strike—the worst industrial conflict of the nineteenth century—was precipitated by a reduction of the company's workforce, along with a thirty percent lowering of wages of those that remained, although stockholders continued to receive dividends. Industrialist George Pullman and his management refused to enter into negotiations with labor; and mediation offered by the Civic Federation's arbitration board led nowhere. In the meantime, the American Railway Union—Eugene Debs's new labor organization that accepted both skilled and unskilled workers—voted to support the strikers.

Pullman had constructed a model town for his workers next to his factory near Lake Calumet, with a population that grew to fourteen thousand. It had an up-to-date infrastructure, impressive landscaping and buildings, as well as good schools, a well-stocked library, a theater, and one of the best sports facilities in the country—with the company in charge of their upkeep. An experiment that drew international attention and many admiring visitors, the town of Pullman was hailed as the creation of an enlightened entrepreneur committed to the moral and social betterment of his employees' lives.

Yet judging by another standard, the town seemed less ideal. Built in order to "turn a profit" in the production of Palace

Sleeping-Cars and other Pullman luxury-cars, it was designed to provide workers who were skilled, productive, sober family-men. And in both his enterprises—town and factory—Pullman exercised near absolute control. In his industrial town, no union activity was allowed. Nor did he permit his employees' houses to be privately-owned; or their rents, already high, to be reduced to offset lower wages during downturns in the economy. Each town service came with a crippling cost for residents.

The "sympathy boycott" of Pullman railway-cars by Debs's industry-wide union caused rail traffic to reach a virtual standstill in over half the nation. As a result, the powerful General Managers' Association entered the conflict on the side of Pullman. Through its influence in Washington, an injunction (judge's order) was obtained to stop the boycott, issued on the grounds that the strike interfered with the delivery of the U.S. mail and violated the Sherman Antitrust Act by restraining trade and commerce. Strike-breakers were brought in, with "toughs" to back them up; and the federal government was persuaded to send in troops.

Not wanting to intervene in the boycott, Governor Altgeld had relied on local and state authorities to control the situation and preserve law and order. It was against his objections that President Cleveland dispatched troops to Chicago—thereby transforming the conflict into one of the federal government versus labor. Violence flared up when the army troops, in defending strike-breakers and taking over rail cars, opened fire. Altogether, some thirty workers were killed while the strike lasted, and many more wounded. The destruction unleashed amounted to over a third of a million dollars—railroad cars burned and tracks, equipment, and buildings severely damaged by strikers under attack and by an unruly mob in the streets.

Within weeks of the army's arrival, the boycott ended in failure for the union. The alliance of management, the courts, and the federal government—along with well-armed troops—proved sufficient to defeat it. For the first time, the 1890 Antitrust Act was used against labor, not business monopolies as intended. Debs was arrested for violating an injunction, given a six months' sentence, and through his reading in prison, converted to socialism. In future years, he organized the Socialist Party of America and ran five times for President on its ticket.

There had been sympathy for the Pullman strikers at the start of the strike, for Pullman's treatment of his impoverished employees was viewed as harsh and extreme. But once violence broke out, the threat of anarchy and class warfare changed middle class perceptions. In contrast, Addams observed "almost everyone on Halsted Street wearing a white ribbon, the emblem of the strikers' side."

Deeply disturbed by events which had spiraled out-of-control, she'd played a major role in trying to bring the opposing parties together. But to no avail. Pullman withdrew to his summer home on the coast of New Jersey in stony silence. Once the strike collapsed, President Cleveland commissioned an investigation into its causes. The findings did not turn out well for Pullman. Because of his unreasonable demands on his employees and his refusal to negotiate with them, he lost his good reputation; and in a state lawsuit brought against him, he was ordered to divest his town properties "for exceeding the terms of their charter." His paternalism was pronounced out-of-step with acceptable public policy.

With her strong literary sense, Addams had expressed her concern over the bitterness and divisiveness of the boycott in an essay comparing George Pullman in the Pullman Strike with King Lear in Shakespeare's tragedy. She called it "The Modern King Lear" and did not succeed in having it published until 1912, given its sharp criticism of Pullman. Most analyses of the strike had been "broadly divided between . . . those who held that the philanthropy of the president of the Pullman Company had been most ungratefully received, and those who maintained that the situation was the inevitable outcome of the social consciousness developing among working people." She focused upon "the inevitable revolt of human nature" against an outdated philanthropy.

As benefactors, both "the royal father [Lear] and the philanthropic president of the Pullman company" had conferred "extraordinary benefits"—Lear upon his favorite daughter Cordelia and Pullman upon his private town of workers. Still, Addams wondered whether in performing their generous acts, they hadn't "lost the power of recognizing good in their beneficiaries." In her words: "Were not both so absorbed in carrying out a personal plan of improvement that they failed to catch the great moral lesson which their times offered them?" Neither Lear nor Pullman understood that a wider "social ethic" had emerged to transcend their narrower individualistic one.

To Lear as a father, it was hard to comprehend that his daughter "should be moved by a principle outside of himself"— that of a fuller life in marriage across the sea in France, beyond his authority. In the same way, Pullman as an employer had no awareness of the new movement that had swept his town—that of unionism with its "watchwords of brotherhood, sacrifice, [and] the subordination of individual and trade interests to the good of the working class." Addams' first of eleven books, *Democracy and Social Ethics* (1905), further examined the theme of individual and social ethics, so central to her thinking.

While the Panic of 1893 and the Pullman Strike of 1894 were taking their toll on Chicago's economy, the landmark Illinois Factory Law regulating work conditions appeared to be unraveling. The bill's most controversial provision—the eight-hour workday for women—was challenged in a court case by the newly formed Illinois Association of Manufacturers, determined to have it rendered unconstitutional.

And in May 1895—in *Richie versus The People*—the State Supreme Court did just that: it issued a verdict against putting any limitations on the work hours of women. Such regulation, it held, was "in excess of the powers of the legislature" as set forth in the Fourteenth Amendment of the *Constitution*:

"No State shall make or enforce any law which shall abridge the privileges or immunities of citizens of the United States; nor shall any State deprive any person of life, liberty, or property, without due process of law . . ."

The next day, an editorial in the *Chicago Tribune* newspaper voiced its approval, declaring that: "[One's] labor is property and an interference with the sale of it . . . is an infringement of a constitutional right to dispose of property." A pro-labor paper, in protest, called the court's notion of employees negotiating the terms of their labor individually with their employers "the relic of a pre-industrial age." Kelley, who had recently completed a law degree at Northwestern University night school, described the reasoning as a "perversion of the historic 1868 amendment."

In the third of her always instructive factory reports, she derided the court for ruling that the amendment to the *Constitution* "passed for the purpose of guaranteeing the Negro from oppression" stood as an "insuperable obstacle to the protection of women and children in industry." Given that justices had acquired the "power to overturn statutes," she foresaw that all effort for social legislation would be in vain if the decision was not overruled. As she viewed it, the verdict enabled employers to obtain the upper hand in court decisions by setting an individual's "freedom of contract," above a state's right to promote its citizens' welfare.

She proceeded to contrast Illinois' Supreme Court decision with the "policy of states and nations where the principle of legislative regulation of work conditions had been accepted and could be acted upon." The care and health of female factory employees was regarded as a legitimate matter for lawmakers "in France, Germany and every other continental country . . . as well as the more progressive states of the United States." And in England, then the "greatest manufacturing nation in the world, a more beneficent social policy toward women and children in industry" had been supported for decades, through a series of Factory Acts passed in Parliament.

The Richie decision stood in disregard, too, of American

judicial precedent. For twenty years, Kelley continued, the constitutionality of Massachusetts's ten hour law regulating the work
of women and children had not been disputed, with New York
following Massachusetts's lead. Yet in Illinois, the third largest
manufacturing state, the "judicial mind hadn't kept pace with the
strides of industrial development."

Ten years later, her book *Some Ethical Gains Through Legislation*
would document the country's "up-and-down" struggle to achieve
civilized work conditions for labor's most vulnerable members.

## Sources

Addams, Jane. *Jane Addams Reader.* "A Modern Lear," Edited by K.
      B. Elshtain. NY: Basic Books, 2002, 163–176.
———. *Twenty Years at Hull-House.* NY: Macmillan, 1973,
      213–221.
Barnard, Harry. *Eagle Forgotten: The Life of John Peter Altgeld.*
      Indianapolis, IN: Bobbs-Merrill, 1938, 280–344.
Elshtain, Jean Bethke. *Jane Addams and the Dream of American
      Democracy: A Life.* NY: Basic Books, 2002, 111–113.
Kelley, Florence. *The Selected Letters of Florence Kelley, 1869–1931.*
      Edited by Kathryn Sklar and Beverly Wilson Palmer. Urbana:
      University of Illinois Press, 2009, xxi–xli.
———. *Some Ethical Gains Through Legislation*, 1905. Online:
      Ebook and Texts Archive, California Digital Library: http://
      www.cdlib.org/
Knight, Louise W. *Jane Addams: Spirit in Action.* NY: W.W.
      Norton, 2010, 86, 88–103.
Miller, Donald L. *City of the Century.* NY: Simon & Schuster,
      1996, 534–551.
Sklar, Kathryn Kish. *Florence Kelley and the Nation's Work.* New
      Haven: Yale University Press, 1995, 257–258, 281–284.
"Hull-House in the 1890s." *Signs*, vol. 10, no. 4 (Summer, 1985),
      University of Chicago Press, 658–677.

# CHAPTER 3

# Jane Addams

The childhood of Jane Addams in the little village of Cedarville, Illinois, bore little resemblance to her life as an adult in the Nineteenth Ward of Chicago. Her early years in the rural northern part of the state after the Civil War were relatively unaffected by the rapid industrialization and influx of immigrants that would transform Chicago. By 1890 the city had become the second largest in the nation, with three-quarters of its one million inhabitants foreign born, or of foreign parentage.

In 1862 at the age of two, Jennie—as she was called—lost her mother in her ninth childbirth. The youngest of five surviving children, she was cared for by her eldest sister Mary until her father remarried five years later. But it was to her father that she gave her wholehearted devotion and affection. As she stated in her autobiography *Twenty Years at Hull-House*: "I centered upon him all that careful imitation which a little girl ordinarily gives to her mother's ways and habits."

For instance, she developed "a consuming ambition to possess a [flattened] miller's thumb" like his, and would sit for long periods "rubbing the ground wheat between her thumb and fingers as it fell from between the millstones on its way to becoming flour." She also had the idea of rising at four a.m., the hour he'd risen as a miller's apprentice and still did by habit. Following his example, she determined to read through the books of the Cedarville library—as he had the collection of his town's library in Pennsylvania. Since the Cedarville books were housed in the Addams' parlor; and since she often chanced to awaken at that untimely hour, she began reading them in chronological order with translations of the *Iliad* and the *Aeneid*—but ended up reducing her program of study to a single book, *The History of the World*.

Of Quaker descent, John Huy Addams had emigrated from Pennsylvania to Illinois in the 1840s, newly married. He rose to be a successful miller, then a banker in nearby Freeport, and ultimately the leading citizen of his community. Elected to the state senate for eight terms, he was a friend of Lincoln's as well as his colleague in the new Republican Party. For Jennie, it was always thrilling when, at her request, her father "took out of his desk a thin packet marked 'Mr. Lincoln's Letters'" . . . addressed to "'My dear Double-D'd Addams.'" With bated breath, she would await his "reminiscences of this wonderful man . . . or even better, that he should be moved to tell some of the exciting incidents of the Lincoln-Douglas debates."

And she remembered, during her eleventh year, entering her father's room one morning and finding him "sitting beside the fire with a newspaper in his hand, looking very solemn." From her questioning, she learned that the Italian Giuseppe Mazzini had died. When she protested that they didn't even know him, she was made aware that a "genuine relationship" could exist between "men who share large hopes and like desires—such as abolishing slavery in America or throwing off Hapsburg oppression in Italy—even though they differed in nationality, language, and creed." That lesson filled her with pride that her father was "a man who held converse with great minds and who really sorrowed and rejoiced over happenings across the sea."

Her father's remarriage when she was eight, added a forceful figure to the household—the widow Anna Haldeman, along with her two sons, the youngest one the age of Jennie. Cultivated, intelligent, and spirited, Anna loved music, the arts, fine clothes and travel. Two memorable family trips came about at her urging—one to Madison, the capital of Wisconsin sixty miles to the north, and the other to the 1876 Centennial Fair in Philadelphia. Unlike the

Addamses, her stepmother had a volatile temperament, making the transition to her authority a difficult one for Jennie, and fostering in her a life-long aversion to confrontation. However Anna did take her stepdaughter's cultural education in hand, while young George became her constant companion.

The two youngsters roamed the countryside together and invented imaginative games and "crusades" that could go on indefinitely—which she later regretted was not possible for tenement children in city streets full of traffic that disrupted their play. In her autobiography, she recalled her and George's response to nature, "when we clapped our hands in sudden joy over the soft radiance of the rainbow" or "yielded to a soft melancholy when we heard the whippoorwill in the early twilight." And she described how the prairie that surrounded the village broke into hills, "one of them crowned by pine woods grown up from a bag full of Norway pine seeds sown by my father." She told, too, of how "the banks of the mill stream rose into high bluffs . . . containing caves of which one at least was so black that it could not be explored without the aid of a candle."

Serious and reflective, Jennie found sustenance in books all her life. As a young girl in Cedarville, she read the biographies of famous men and heroes recommended by her father, along with the works of Dickens, George Eliot, and Emerson, which stood out among her own favorites. She read articles on social reformers as well—many from the *Atlantic Monthly* that Anna subscribed to. Her dream was to attend Smith, the recently opened New England women's college offering a Bachelor of Arts degree comparable to that of men's colleges. Her father, though, wanted her closer to home at Rockford Seminary, where he'd been a trustee and her older sisters had gone. She could finish her schooling, he said, with a European tour. For the first time, what she referred to as the "family claim" stood in opposition to her desire to take advantage of an opportunity beyond familial ties.

Once established at Rockford Seminary, Jane, as she chose to be known in college, blossomed—excelling in her courses, recognized as a leader by her classmates, and prized as a student by her teachers. Yet she failed to respond to the headmistress Miss Sill's proselytizing for missionary service. Her church in Cedarville had been non-denominational; and as a Quaker her father was not doctrinaire. As she explained it: "I suppose I held myself aloof from these [evangelical] influences, partly owing to the fact that my father was not a communicant of any church, and I tremendously admired his scrupulous morality and sense of honor in all matters of personal and public conduct." She struggled to be true to his counsel to "be honest with yourself inside, whatever happens."

One inspiring teacher, Caroline Potter—a relative of Julia Lathrop's—introduced her to "female heroes" in history, from the Egyptian goddess Isis to the recently deceased French novelist George Sand. Thereafter, in student essays, debates, and the college's literary magazine, she drew upon themes and material from her readings of great women. Her junior class oration "Bread Givers" presented a subject she would continue to explore—that of the age-old tradition of a woman's work and mission as bread-giver. In her senior essay "Cassandra," she probed the tragic fate of the ancient Trojan princess whose intuitive mind enabled her to see into the future . . . but was "always disbelieved and rejected."

Addams graduated as valedictorian of her class in 1881; and when the Seminary became a college in 1882, she was called back to be awarded a B.A. for her outstanding academic achievement. Early on, she'd settled upon medicine as a career, one where she would live among the poor. In her senior year, her future plans took form—first, to acquire more of a background in science at Smith, and then to attend medical school in Scotland. But for a second time her father intervened to prevent her from pursuing her ambition. Once more the "family claim" took precedence over the course of action she'd set for herself. And then came the most devastating blow of all—her father's death at age fifty-nine from a ruptured appendix. Eight frustrating years of indecision and inaction followed. Ill health and ongoing family obligations, especially to her stepmother, contributed to her trials.

An orphan and still coming to grips with the loss of her father, she managed to complete a term at the Women's Medical School in Philadelphia, before withdrawing from stress, severe back pain, and the realization that she wasn't suited for the field of medicine. Surgery for a crooked spine kept her in bed for six months—her only compensation being a return to the reading of history and literature. A trip to Europe with her stepmother and a few others, part as recovery and part in pursuit of culture, enabled her to visit museums and cathedrals, attend opera and concerts, and behold the sites of the literary world that had been so influential in her education. But she experienced another side of Europe as well—acute poverty. At a Saturday night "auction" of decaying food that grew cheaper by the hour until the market closed at midnight, she viewed first-hand "the hideous human need and suffering of East London."

In Rome she became interested in the Catacombs as a democratic interpretation of Christianity, one in which it was the poor who took its message to "the more prosperous Romans." The simplicity of life that characterized the primitive church in a community which put aside class divisions, contrasted sharply with her own privileged existence. She was left "clinging to the desire to live in a really living world and refusing to be content with a shadowy intellectual or academic reflection of it." Back in America, she stayed with Anna for the winter months in Baltimore where her stepbrother was studying biology at Johns Hopkins; and much to Anna's displeasure, turned down George's marriage proposal. Then in the summer she was baptized in the Presbyterian Church of Cedarville—from a weariness over her failures at "self-dependence" and a longing for "an outward symbol of fellowship." In 1887 she returned to Europe with her college friend Ellen Gates Starr, and paid a much-anticipated visit to Toynbee Hall as a preliminary step to their opening such a settlement in a poor section of Chicago.

—⁊ ⁊—

Flexibility and a readiness to experiment were pivotal to Hull-House's becoming the most famous settlement in the country. Initially benevolence and good will had motivated the two founders—who welcomed and celebrated the cultural diversity of the Nineteenth Ward. And it was with genuine feeling that Addams responded to the conflict between generations that immigrant families experienced—and which she'd known herself. Activities offered by the settlement soon encompassed urgent and felt needs expressed by the neighbors themselves. Attempts to deal with tenement living and the industrial system inevitably led to involvement with civic organizations and city government. It required spending "many hours in efforts to secure support for deserted women, insurance for bewildered widows, damages for injured [machine] operators, [and] furniture from the clutches of the installment store."

At times tragedy resulted from the crushing demands placed on mothers like "Goosie's"— a child first "brought to the nursery wrapped up in his mother's shawl . . . his hair filled with the down and small feathers from the brush factory where she worked." A few years later while she was hanging out an early morning wash on the shed roof, as Addams tells it:

> Five-year-old Goosie was trotting at her heels handing her clothespins, when he was suddenly blown off the roof by the strong wind into the alley below. His neck was broken by the fall and as he lay piteous and limp on a pile of frozen refuse, his mother cheerily called him to "climb up again," so confident do overworked mothers become that their children cannot get hurt.

Another neighborhood child, an Italian girl named Carlotta with "haunting black eyes," labored long hours with her family making artificial flowers for women's hats. Her father had died of consumption; and in their dark, damp flat without warmth or adequate food, Carlotta developed the same illness. Soon she followed her father to the grave, "her frail little body in a small white-velvet-covered coffin," her "weeping mother supported by Jane Addams who had placed a small bouquet of real flowers on the coffin."

And when it was discovered that the ward's Democrat party boss Johnny Powers was using the job of garbage inspector as a "political plum"—accounting for the filthy conditions in the neighborhood streets and alleys—Addams applied successfully to be garbage inspector herself. After she'd followed the contractors' trucks on their daily rounds for a few months, the situation changed for the better; and a Hull-House resident replaced her as regular inspector. But it set off an all-out fight with Powers—which he won by exerting his influence to have the inspector's job consolidated with another in a nearby district, held by a crony.

Further efforts to defeat Powers as alderman of the Nineteenth Ward proved futile. Wielding the power he'd built up over the years, he put large numbers of his allies on the city payroll and delivered personal favors to constituents for their votes. Addams applied what pressure she could at city hall and extended her reform activities—gaining the reputation of a defender of the labor movement. While such a stance aggravated many of Chicago's wealthy citizens who were Hull-House donors, Addams nevertheless continued to support organized labor, particularly women's labor, and to uphold workers' right to form unions.

Her ability to attract capable people brought a remarkable group of individuals to the settlement. Perhaps no more admirable and gifted women could have been assembled anywhere than the six of Addams, Julia Lathrop, Florence Kelley, Alice Hamilton, and Edith and Grace Abbott. Working together, they fought selflessly and tirelessly for social justice. Kelley began her residency by instigating an anti-sweatshop campaign, while Lathrop dedicated her early efforts to the reform of state charity institutions, Hamilton to combatting industrial disease, Edith Abbott to social research, and Grace Abbott to newly-arrived immigrants. But it was Addams' steady hand at the helm of Hull-House that united these distinctive personalities in pursuing common goals.

## *Sources*

Addams, Jane. *The Social Thought of Jane Addams*. Edited by
     Christopher Lasch. Indianapolis: Bobbs-Merrill Company,
     1965, xv-xvii, 12-28.

———. *Twenty Years at Hull-House*. NY: Macmillan Publishing
     Company, 1938. First published 1910. 11–47, 173–174.

Elshtain, Jean Bethke. *Jane Addams and the Dream of American
     Democracy*. NY: Basic Books, 2002, 33–37, 48–51, 55–57,
     61–62.

Knight, Louise W. *Jane Addams: Spirit in Action*. NY: Norton &
     Company, 2010. chapters 1–2.

*Notable American Women: Biographical Dictionary*, vol. 1. Edited by
     Edward James. Cambridge: Ralph Fletcher Seymour, 1946,
     s.v. "Addams, Jane."

Polachaeck, Hilda Satt. *I Came a Stranger*. Urbana: University of
     Illinois Press, 1989, 53–54.

# Hull-House Children

*Kindergartners with teacher.*

*Swing.*

*Violin lesson.*

*Girl glazing pottery made in Hull-House kiln.*

"The arts have, I think, always been embodied in the ultimate aims of Hull-House." — *Jane Addams*

*At a Hull-House recital.*

*Boy sketching.*

# Bowen Country Club

*Boy smelling flowers.*

*Girl with pinwheel.*

*Dance tableau.*

*In the pottery class.*

*Hull-House boys' band.*

*Former Hull-House boy Benny Goodman playing clarinet for Hull-House children.*

"Of all the modes of artistic expression, the one with perhaps the most universal appeal is the drama. Certainly we at Hull-House have found no other means so successful in holding a large group together from childhood, through adolescence and into maturity."
— *Edith de Nancrede, dramatics director*

*Teen actors striking a pose.*

# CHAPTER 4

# Julia Lathrop

While Jane Addams and Julia Lathrop had similar backgrounds, the direction their individual lives took differed. As Addams expressed it in her 1935 biography of Lathrop, *My Friend Julia Lathrop*: "Writing the book was like rewriting my own autobiography from a different angle."

In terms of family and birthplace, they had much in common. Both spent their formative years in nearby counties in northern Illinois, were daughters of pioneer families that had migrated from the East, and had fathers who became important men in their community and in state government.

The eldest of five children—two girls and three boys—Julia Lathrop was born in 1858 to William Lathrop, a lawyer and advocate of women's rights; and Sarah Potter, valedictorian of Rockford Seminary's first graduating class. In the state legislature, Lathrop authored the bill that permitted women to practice law in Illinois; and he prepared the first female admitted to the bar by supervising her reading. Both parents approved of their daughter's desire to attend Vassar, the first of the new women's colleges.

Rockford, where the Lathrops settled and Julia returned to live with her widowed sister after her retirement, was situated on the Rock River midway between Chicago and Galena. With the river's hydraulic power and the arrival of the Galena & Chicago Union Railroad in 1852, the town developed into a machine-and-tool manufacturing center. By the seventies, Swedish immigrants began to make their mark among the city's inventors and entrepreneurs, rising initially through the furniture industry. By the mid-1920s, they controlled some fifty of Rockford's industrial establishments and accounted for about a third of the population.

A distinguished attorney and reformer, Lathrop was known for his "flashing wit and the ability suddenly to give a brilliant turn to the situation under discussion"—as was his daughter Julia in her settlement years and later in Washington. She also resembled her father in her lifelong commitment to the merit system in civil service appointments. Since party politics rather than fitness for a position regularly determined who would be appointed with each change of administration, civil service reform was a critical issue. As a Republican representative in Congress, Lathrop was an early supporter of reform to eliminate the "spoils system." And he set an example himself, backing up his convictions in one instance by selecting a West Point cadet on the basis of a competitive examination.

The first Lathrop ancestor to arrive in America—Reverend John Lothropp—would have set sail on the Mayflower, Julia once remarked at Hull-House, except that he was in jail at the time, having been arrested as the minister of a nonconformist congregation in London. Julia's father, too, held liberal religious views; yet in consideration of his wife's strong beliefs, he attended the Congregational Church as head of the family until his children reached an age to decide on church membership themselves. To their mother's regret, none became church members when they reached the appropriate age. A prominent place in the household was accorded by both parents to books: Mrs. Lathrop belonged to a women's reading club, Mr. Lathrop singled out book-buying as the one "extravagance" allowed his children, and "books and reading served as his own greatest recreation." Dramatics played a role in the family as well, with Julia directing the younger children in scripts she made up for their entertainment.

After a year at Rockford Seminary, she transferred to Vassar where she designed her own "disciplinary training," studying courses like statistics, institutional history, and community organization in the growing field of social science. Upon graduation in 1880, she was welcomed as secretary into her father's law office, read law, and "knew a great deal about it," in the words of her oldest brother who'd become his father's law partner. But given the barriers to entering male-dominated occupations, it was not until she joined Hull-House in its second year, 1890, that settlement work provided her with the pathway to a fulfilling career.

From the start, she found "communal living utterly satisfying." Possessing the "settlement spirit," she thrived in living among her peers in a working-class immigrant neighborhood. With her lively sense of humor, ready wit, and "gift for friendship," she established a special rapport with the new residents, who she treated with genuine respect and understanding. Her empathy for others made her a natural mediator, trusted for her fairness and admired for her judgment. Jane Addams praised her "disinterested virtue," her "unfailing sense of moral obligation," and her deep-rooted compassion. She readily became one of the "inner circle" of Hull-House reformers of the 1890s—along with Addams and Kelley and, towards the end of the decade, Alice Hamilton.

One of her first settlement endeavors was the Sunday afternoon Plato Club, a neighborhood philosophical discussion group of mainly older Greek men who read Plato and held definite ideas about the "purpose of the universe." From time to time University of Chicago professor John Dewey took part in the club's far-ranging discussions. A few years later, Hull-House resident Edith Abbott described Lathrop's sympathetic response to a much younger Greek in the neighborhood:

> I well remember one very early summer morning, almost dawn, when she called some sleeping residents of Hull-House to a front window in the hall. We looked out to see walking down Halsted Street a young Greek in the white kilted skirt of Hellas, tasseled slippers and a tasseled cap, piping very musically on some long reed-like instrument. The lad was evidently on his way home from a national festival of some kind. But Miss Lathrop had

been so moved by the wistful, homesick figure and the flutelike melody that floated through the still morning air that she said: "When I looked out of the window I gradually saw the Attic plains stretching out there where last night we saw only the sordidness of Halsted Street.

She had the unusual habit of sleeping in the early evening and waking up when most residents went to bed. This meant that she would read and write long into the night, before finishing her sleep. Although housework didn't interest her, she'd mastered a dish of browned buttered oysters that was always a treat when prepared for Sunday supper at the settlement. Maple ice cream was another specialty of hers, a dessert her great-niece recalled among childhood memories of her aunt.

Lathrop first participated in public welfare work during the Panic of 1893–1894, when she volunteered to interview impoverished neighbors who'd applied for assistance from the County Welfare Agency. It was during that dreadful winter, Addams reported, "that I first saw fully revealed Julia Lathrop's profound human pity for her helpless fellow men, her responsibility for basic human needs which afforded so much of the driving power back of her splendid abilities." She was assigned to visit applicants in the ten blocks surrounding Hull-House.

Upon being elected Democratic governor in 1892, Altgeld opened up opportunities for women by placing them on state boards and in supervisory positions for children and women. Thus Kelley became head Factory Inspector for Illinois and Lathrop was made a member of the State Board of Charities. For twelve years she traveled from one end of the state to the other, investigating the one-hundred and two county poorhouses and farms, never failing to consult with the inmates themselves to see things from their point of view. Her recommendations included separate institutions for children, the mentally ill, prisoners, and the infirm; specialized training for nurses and attendants; state rather than county mental hospitals; and occupational therapy for patients. In the selection of administrators and staff, she pressed for a merit system that would be comprehensive in scope.

Alice Hamilton, a Hull-House colleague who accompanied her on one of her visits to an asylum "down-state," gained a valuable lesson from Lathrop's skillful handling of its director. In the words of Dr. Hamilton, a key figure in industrial medicine:

> We were met by the Superintendent who was sulky and suspicious. He did however conduct us all over his establishment and gradually under the influence of Miss Lathrop's cordial and uncritical attitude he thawed out; and presently he was pouring out all his troubles to her, going out of his way to point out what was wrong . . . By the time we had returned to the office he was in a softened and almost mellow mood and I, full of admiration for her skillful handling of a difficult situation, expected her to depart leaving behind this friendly atmosphere.

> But I learned my lesson then. Miss Lathrop sat down in the office and proceeded gently but with devastating thoroughness to go over the whole situation and point out to the superintendent that after all he was the one in authority; if things were rotten it was he who must shoulder the responsibility . . . We left him evidently impressed and promising to do his best, certainly not resentful in spite of her severity.

And Addams recalled another example of that "wonderful method of hers which people call diplomacy but which was really a technique founded upon an understanding of human nature." It happened coming back from the 1900 Paris World's Fair, in a ship with many immigrants in steerage. As Addams related it:

> The coarse black bread which was given the immigrant passengers . . . had become filled with a green mould which made it certainly unpalatable and probably dangerous. A committee of desperate immigrants who

had complained in vain to lesser officials, finally made their way to the captain's bridge holding samples of the green bread in their hands. Unfortunately the burly captain was so enraged by this indignity and breach of ship discipline that he almost threw the panic stricken petitioners into the sea . . . During the next hour the complaint and samples of the bread reached Julia Lathrop, who took up the matter and . . . by evening had secured the promise from the Captain himself that fresh bread should be baked for the immigrants every day.

When the steerage passengers discovered who was behind the fresh bread, Lathrop couldn't walk on deck without being "greeted with a volley of polyglot cheers."

In addition to trying to take partisan politics out of the care of the mentally ill and replacing it with competent training for care-givers, she was interested in the progress of mental hospitals abroad. During European trips of 1898 and 1900, she studied the treatment of patients in the "boarding out" system. Both in Scotland and a few countries on the continent, there had been "a growing recognition of the fact that a large proportion [of the afflicted] could be cared for more economically, more humanely and pleasantly, in a colony or village life or by boarding in families, than in great institutions." Since medieval times, Gheel in Belgium had placed patients with families where they worked in the fields alongside them, or in the village if needed and able. A new "boarding colony" in Belgium had opened up successfully in recent years, two in France, and several near Berlin, with the oversight of directors that included medical and public officials.

A little over a decade later in New York, Lathrop would be the sole woman among "twelve charter members present at the Founding Meeting of the National Committee for Mental Hygiene." The establishment of the Mental Hygiene Society represented a high-point in her search for more humane and effective ways to care for the mentally ill, especially those "in need of skilled services but not necessarily of hospitalization if their families could be instructed to care for them." As a result of her investigations, she felt that nursing carried out under the guidance of experts in psychiatry could "have a preventive effect."

In 1908, Clifford Beers had published his personal account of suffering a three year psychosis inside mental institutions in Connecticut. His book—*The Mind That Found Itself*—drew considerable attention to his experience, to the deplorable conditions that existed, and to the struggle of those plagued by mental illness.

At the Chicago branch of the Mental Hygiene Society, where Lathrop became active, a friend recalled her words when she lingered to talk with a few members after a Sunday evening meeting. The subject being discussed was "what each one would rather do if she were free from all restrictions and obligations." The hostess expressed her desire to defeat a congressman who'd thwarted her favorite projects. Julia Lathrop, when it was her turn to speak, said that under such conditions what she would choose to do would be to "keep a boarding house for the mentally ill."

Then, in 1899, she played a crucial role in enacting a historic piece of welfare legislation for children—the Illinois Juvenile Court Law, the first of its kind in the world. It signaled a positive change in how the law dealt with delinquent children, viewing the child as "in need of help rather than as a criminal to be punished." Together with Lucy Flower of the Chicago Women's Club, Julia Lathrop was the "moving spirit" of the juvenile court movement, which created a probation system for children in trouble with the law. And as a respected member of the Illinois Board of Charities, she was in a position to influence prominent board members into steering a child's court bill through the all-male state legislature.

The city's Women's Club had been seeking solutions for the problem of the dependent and delinquent child since the 1880s. In police stations and jails, club members had managed to introduce women as matrons, operate a school for juveniles serving sentences, and arrange for speedy trials to keep under-age offenders from being held with hardened criminals. As mothers and protectors of family life themselves, they were especially worried about the well-being of immigrant children in the slum, who were often left to fend for themselves on the streets while their parents labored long hours in sweatshops and factories. A number of Hull-House reformers with a background in social science had undertaken to investigate the history of young lawbreakers in the Nineteenth Ward, to assist judges in determining how to help them. Several of the settlement's residents acted as de facto probation officers.

But expectations for the juvenile court, once it had been established, became tempered with time, as the judges' legal training proved unequal to the demands placed upon them. More than the authority of the court and a "personal talk were required to treat the "mental and emotional" as well as" social and economic" causes of individual delinquents' behavior. Moreover passage of the Juvenile Court Bill didn't mean that it was funded. A Juvenile Court Committee formed by Flower and headed, first by Lathrop and then by Louise de Koven Bowen, set about raising money for the salaries of the court's first probation officers, and for operating a detention home until the county would be able to take it over. When the committee had been transformed into the Juvenile Protection Association, it was instrumental in providing a clinic for repeated child offenders—which developed into the Illinois State Institute for Juvenile Research.

Reflecting a quarter of a century later, at a time when most states in the country had set up courts for children, Lathrop said in an interview:

> Anyone who has studied the children brought into juvenile courts realizes that a large part of juvenile delinquency is due to grinding poverty. It is at the basis of our social problem.

## *Sources*

Abbott, Grace. *The Child and the State.* Chicago: University of Chicago Press, 1938, part II, introduction.

Addams, Jane, *My Friend, Julia Lathrop.* Urbana: University of Illinois Press, 2004, 17–24, 33–37, 45–46, 60–2. See also "Introduction" by Anne Firor Scott, x–xvii.

Clapp, Elizabeth J. "The Chicago Juvenile Court Movement in the 1890s." Article given as a paper at the Centre for Urban History, University of Leicester, March 1995.

Lathrop, Julia C. "The Isolation of our Public Charities." *The Commons*, Dec., 1901.

Lundin, Jon V. *Rockford: An Illustrated History.* Chatsworth California: Windsor Publications, 1989, 17, 42–47, 67–74.

Mennel, Robert. *Thorns and Thistles: Juvenile Delinquency in the United States, 1825–1940.* Hannover NH: University Press of New England, 1973, chapter 5.

Muncy, Robyn. *Creating a Female Dominion in American Reform.* NY: Oxford University Press, 1991, 32–33.

# Florence Kelley

F lorence Kelley was born in 1859 and lived "four miles as the crow flies from Independence Hall" in Philadelphia. Her father William Kelley, elected to the United States House of Representatives for fourteen terms, shared his "passion for politics" with her in long talks at home and informative letters from Washington. Committed to a high tariff to protect the iron and steel industries, he reasoned that a better life for all would result from strong industrial growth—a judgment he later had to reassess.

Descended from Scotch-Irish Protestants of Northern Ireland, who arrived in New Jersey in the 1660s, William was raised by his mother after his father's death when the boy was an infant. At eleven he left school to contribute to the family income provided by his mother's boarding-house—working first in a printing company and then, following an apprenticeship, as a jeweler like his father had been. In time he read law, was admitted to the bar, and served as a judge for ten years in Philadelphia, gaining a reputation as an orator and a defender of working men, women's rights, and the emancipation of slaves. Democracy, he came to believe, required a strong central government to afford protection to all citizens and provide opportunity to the children of the nation through public schools.

An abolitionist, he supported Abraham Lincoln for the presidency, and was elected to the House himself in 1860 as a Republican from a working-class district. In the 1870s and 1880s, Elizabeth Stanton and Susan Anthony counted on him as a champion of woman's suffrage and chairman of Women's Rights Conventions held in the Capital. He met his wife Caroline Bonsall at the Unitarian church of Philadelphia. Orphaned at nine, she had Unitarian-Quaker roots and lived with the Quaker parents who'd adopted her—the Pughs—and her aunt Sarah Pugh in the peaceful Germantown section of the city.

Of eight Kelley children, six girls and two boys, five little girls died young, victims of now preventable childhood diseases. One illness—summer diarrhea—became a leading cause of infant deaths in the country, striking children of all classes through "contaminated food, milk, or water." Three Kelley daughters were lost during the warm weather months. "Florrie" herself was prone to infections, and suffered rheumatism and scarlet fever along with eyestrain, so that she attended school irregularly. For her mother Caroline, all this misfortune combined with her own parents' untimely deaths created a "permanent terror of impending loss," which caused her only surviving daughter to mature at an early age.

It further caused Florrie to draw closer to her father, who she later described as teaching her to read at age seven from "a terrible little book with woodcuts of children no older than myself, balancing with their arms heavy loads of wet clay on their heads, in brickyards in England." During long congressional sessions when he was away, she read widely in his library; and, on trips to Washington, she spent time exploring the Library of Congress. When he was home, he spoke with her about social problems, especially those of children—whether young laborers in Britain, child slaves in the South, indentured boys and girls who'd come to America from England, or his own struggling youth.

The family traveled to the Allegheny Mountains during her twelfth year, after the crushing blow of a fifth child's death. There Florrie learned about the new Bessemer process of turning molten iron into steel, which revolutionized the steel industry. It was a night visit—a "terrifying sight," she reported. But what amazed her even more than the "fireworks display" of the big blast furnaces was the sight of small boys "carrying heavy pails of water and tin dippers," running back and forth in the dark to give the overheated, overworked men a drink.

That same autumn she made another night visit with her father, this time to a glass factory where many children risked their lives as "blowers' dogs," huddled between the workers and the fiery ovens. It was their job "to take a blower's mold the instant the bottle or tumbler was removed from it, scrape and replace it perfectly smooth and clean for the next bottle or tumbler" already on its way. Again, there seemed to be no attention paid to the dangers the little boys were exposed to in such a hazardous industry—in this case, heat, broken glass, and burning.

William Kelley tried to explain to his daughter that it was the duty of his generation "to build up great industries in America so that more wealth could be produced for the whole people." It would be the duty of her generation, he said, to provide for a just distribution of the goods produced. He did not believe that one generation could do both. In the 1880s, though, he lost confidence in the Republican Party with its lopsided defense of capital over labor—and voiced his support for an eight-hour workday as a significant step towards securing decent working conditions.

Some of the happiest memories of Florrie's childhood involved her Quaker grandparents and her great-aunt Sarah in Germantown. Above all, Aunt Sarah stood as an inspiration to her and a source of stories of a proud dissenting past. At fifty she'd given up teaching to devote herself "to promoting the anti-slavery movement, peace, woman's suffrage, the single standard of morals for men and women, and free trade." A longtime president of the city's Female Anti-Slavery Society, the first abolitionist organization in Pennsylvania to have black members, she supported "the radical goal of immediate, uncompensated abolition."

It was her good friend, the activist Lucretia Mott, who presented a resolution at the national convention of anti-slavery women to boycott slave-made merchandise—which passed in 1837. Aunt Sarah refused to eat sugar or wear cotton all her life, as both were products of slave labor. Such a personal protest against the inhumane conditions under which goods were made was a precursor to similar boycotts in the first decades of the twentieth century by the National Consumers League. As its General Secretary for thirty years, Florence (her adult name) led the battle against goods created by child labor, traveling throughout the country—speaking in schools, women's clubs, trade unions, churches, and legislatures.

In 1876 at age sixteen, her formal training began when she entered Cornell, a land grant college offering "equal intellectual opportunity to women." While applying herself wholeheartedly to academic work, she also was able to enjoy the companionship of a circle of friends that made college life "one continued joy." The elective system at the school meant that she could add courses in law, economics, and politics to her Liberal Arts program of languages and literature. And she became actively involved in the founding of a Social Science Club, designed to further open discussion of "all live questions social, moral and political."

Due to illness, she was forced to leave college for over two years—recuperating much of the time in Washington with her father, where she worked on her senior thesis in the Library of Congress. Its subject—"Some Changes in the Legal Status of the Child Since Blackstone"— traced a father's "vested right" in his children in mid-eighteenth century English law, to child welfare through legislation in her own time. Patriarchal power decreased, she found, as children were dealt with as individuals and provided education and protection by the state. Her paper received an Honorable Mention and later appeared in a respected New York periodical, the *International Review*.

Upon receiving her degree, she was denied entry to graduate studies at the University of Pennsylvania to prepare for law school and a legal career. But another project presented itself at Philadelphia's New Century Club, a women's organization committed to women's needs. There she was instrumental in establishing evening courses and a Working Women's Guild that offered "mutual help, enjoyment, and encouragement in high endeavor"—drawing a record number of members. Besides teaching history classes, she served as librarian of the guild with the responsibility of selecting its books.

This undertaking involving middle- and working-class women came to a sudden end for Florence when she was called upon to accompany her older brother Will, who'd fallen ill, to the Riviera for a cure prescribed by the doctor. In Avignon, he was struck by "temporary blindness" and it was largely on her own that she nursed him that winter. Her dedication yielded results, for he showed marked improvement by spring. One highlight during her "family service" to Will was a visit from Carey Thomas, a Cornell graduate (and future president of Bryn Mawr College) who'd acquired a PhD from the University of Zurich, Switzerland—the only university in Europe to grant higher degrees to women.

With her brother sufficiently recovered, the whole Kelley family met in London in the summer. Florence and her father spent time touring industrial areas in South Wales and the Midlands, where they witnessed some horrifying sights—scenes of "women and girls [at] the mouth of coal pits, loading and hauling cars filled with coal;" mothers in miserable huts hammering nails and chains for endless hours of sweat labor; and "diminutive men and women in the streets of the textile manufacturing cities," shriveled and prematurely-gray.

It was decided that she would pursue graduate study at the University of Zurich; and in the fall she enrolled as a student of government, with a focus on history and economics. Her mother and younger brother Albert moved to Zurich with her, which had a sizeable American colony and a number of women foreign students in the medical school—half of them Russian.

A picturesque university town on the Limmat River, Zurich was known as a refuge for European socialists. Many Social Democrat leaders and party members, driven from Germany by Bismarck's 1878 Antisocialist Law, settled in the city and conducted regular meetings there. At her first socialist gathering, Florence encountered a very different conception of protective tariffs than her father's—that of the international obligation of workers to each other. According to such a conception, a tariff to improve the standard of living of one country should not create "a lowering of the standard of living of fellow workers on the other side of the globe." The idealism expressed in such a view—she later wrote in an autobiographical sketch— reminded her of Quaker meetings in Germantown.

On New Year's Day 1884, Lazare Wischnewetzky, a Russian-Jewish medical student she'd met in her political economy class, paid a formal visit to Florence, her mother, and brother. A declared socialist, he shared many of her interests and treated her as an intellectual equal. Even her mother grew to consider the two as "congenial spirits." By June they were married; and in October she became a socialist herself—a member of the German Social Democratic Party. She also translated Engels's *Condition of the Working Class in England in 1844*—his first important book.

Written when Engels was twenty-four, it included "a historical account of the development of capitalism," based on official British reports and his own observation of the dire poverty of industrial workers. To Florence, his moral indignation at their working conditions resembled that of her father and great-aunt Sarah toward slavery. Her correspondence with Engels, which began in 1884, lasted for ten years.

Upon her return back home in the fall of 1886, with her husband and one-year-old son, the letters reveal her disillusionment with an insular, German-speaking socialist party in America—and with a Federation of Labor focused on negotiating with employers rather than forming a vibrant political party. Engels, in turn, was skeptical of her reliance on middle-class women's groups. His "scientific socialism" held economic forces to be the determining factor of social change.

During five years in New York City, Florence's activities shifted increasingly from socialist theory to the welfare of working women and children. With her pen, she attacked child labor in a series of forceful articles, drawing on both state documents and personal experience as Engels had done in his analysis of capitalism forty years earlier. In one "hard-hitting" study, "Our Toiling Children," she dealt in explicit detail with the unrelieved misery of child wage-earners, their lack of education, and the scarcity of information in state and federal bureaus about their plight.

Meanwhile her husband's medical practice had proven incapable of supporting a family of, by then, three little children, despite repeated help from Florence's father and his investment in Lazare's Mechanico-Therapeutic Institute. Using the Zander technique developed in Sweden, the Institute provided exercises "to correct posture and improve muscle tone" by means of an involved system of mechanical equipment. Faced with the failure of the Institute and mounting debts, the marriage disintegrated, ending in his physical abuse of her. Two days after Christmas in 1891, she packed "two trunks of clothes," borrowed money for train fare to Chicago, and left for good, with six-year-old Nikolas, five-year-old Margaret, and three-year-old John.

In Chicago she headed for the hotel of the Women's Temperance Union, whose editor had published her article on the nation's toiling children. With her own youngsters settled in the Union's nursery the following day, she made her way to Hull-House. As she described it:

> On a snowy morning between Christmas 1891 and New Year's 1892, I arrived at Hull-House, Chicago, a little before breakfast time, and found there Henry Standing Bear, a Kickapoo Indian, waiting for the front door to be opened. It was Miss Addams who opened it, holding on her left arm a singularly unattractive, fat, pudgy baby belonging to the cook, who was behindhand with breakfast. Miss Addams was a little hindered in her movements by a super-energetic kindergarten child, left by its mother while she went to a sweat-shop for a bundle of cloaks to be finished . . .

We were welcomed as though we had been invited. We stayed, Henry Standing Bear as helper to the engineer several months, when he returned to his tribe; and I resident seven happy, active years . . .

In a subsequent letter to her mother, she informed her:

> We are all well, and the chicks are happy. I have fifty dollars a month and my board and shall have more soon as I can collect my wits enough to write. I have charge of the Bureau of Labor of Hull-House here and am working in the lines which I have always loved. I do not know what more to tell you except this, that in the few weeks of my stay here I have won for the children and myself many and dear friends whose generous hospitality astonishes me.

Addams and Kelley experienced an immediate rapport. Julia Lathrop recognized that from the start the two women "understood each other's powers"—which allowed them to join forces in "a wonderfully effective way." And as an adult, Kelley's eldest son Nikolas (Ko) reported that "from the time my mother first went to Hull-House until her death, more than forty years later, she looked upon Miss Addams as her dearest and most intimate friend . . . and admired her and approved of her unreservedly."

A significant portion of his formative years were spent at Hull-House, as well as the home of the social critic Henry Demarest Lloyd and boarding "in the suburbs" with the mother of Frank Lloyd Wright. Thinking of those days, although his own mother was often gone for weeks on end as factory inspector, Nikolas felt he'd been "blessed with the best bringing up and educating of anybody that I have known of my time."

At Hull-House as he remembered it, "every day held an adventure of some kind," and life was lived "at a high pitch." Among the residents who made an impression on him was the athletic young Mackenzie King, future prime minister of the Liberal Party in Canada; while special dinner guests might include the activist attorney Clarence Darrow, University of Chicago philosopher John Dewey, or Illinois governor John Altgeld.

As a memorable experience, he singled out a visit with his mother's assistant to one of the May 1886 Haymarket Bombing defendants, convicted of killing a policeman during labor agitation for an eight-hour day. Of eight men prosecuted as conspirators, four were hanged, another committed suicide, and three received life sentences—but were later pardoned by Governor Altgeld as having undergone a "serious miscarriage of justice."

A review of the trial by Altgeld produced no solid evidence linking the defendants to the bomb. Its actual thrower was never identified. The governor concluded that the men had been condemned "not because they were proven guilty of murder, but because they were anarchists." To Nikolas, the "gentle-spoken, thin little cobbler [he met] . . . seemed more likely to be of the philosophical than of the bomb-throwing school of anarchists."

The highly polarized pardons ended Altgeld's political career—and as a result, Kelley's tenure as industrial inspector in Illinois. The impact of the "Haymarket Affair" set the labor movement back for decades. For Kelley, the loss of her job brought her Hull-House period to a close two years later when a new position opened up for her in New York.

## Sources

Barnard, Harry. *Eagle Forgotten: The Life of John Peter Altgeld.*
   Indianapolis, IN: Bobbs-Merrill, 1938, 203–267.

Blumberg, Dorothy. *Florence Kelley.* NY: Augustus Kelley
   Publishers, 1966, 13, 16–20, 26–31, 34–41, 44–46, 99–107,
   125–130, 146–148, and chapters 2, 4, 9.

Goldmark, Josephine. *Impatient Crusader.* Urbana: University of
   Illinois Press, 1953, Foreword and chapters 1–3.

Kelly, Florence. *The Selected Letters of Florence Kelley, 1869–1931.*
   Edited by Kathryn Sklar and Beverly Wilson Palmer. Urbana:
   University of Illinois Press, 2009, 1–5, 498.

Kelley, Nicolas. "Early Days at Hull House." From a speech at the
    Sixty-fifth Annual Meeting of Hull-House, 1954.

Sklar, Kathryn Kish. *Florence Kelley and the Nation's Work*. New
    Haven: Yale University Press, 1995, 50–52, 63–68,75–82,
    86–90, 118–121, and chapters 1–2, 7–8.

Zeisler, Sigmund. "Reminiscences of the Anarchist Case,"
    *Commercial Law League Journal*, December 1926, 553–564.

# CHAPTER 6

# Hull-House Maps and Papers

Kelley, in four autobiographical sketches—"My Philadelphia," "When Coeducation Was Young," "My Novitiate" (conversion to socialism), and "I Go To Work"—related the background to her lifelong struggle for reform on behalf of laboring women and children. In the final sketch, she spoke of directing the Chicago part of a 1893 federal study on the slums of great cities. With a group of inquiry-men under her guidance, she canvassed "a square mile extending from Hull-House on the west to State Street on the east, and several long blocks south." It included people of eighteen nationalities.

Results of the investigation were published in 1894 in a United States Labor Department report *The Slums of Baltimore, Chicago, New York, and Philadelphia*. The next year the innovative *Hull-House Maps and Papers* appeared, which evolved from the study. It was subtitled: *a presentation of nationalities and wages in a congested district of Chicago, together with comments and essays on problems growing out of the social conditions.*

Insightfully written by Hull-House residents—including Addams, Kelley, Lathrop, and Starr—along with a few others, the book featured color-coded maps of ethnicity and income in the poorest immigrant neighborhood of the city. A forerunner to it was Charles Booth's *Life and Labour of the People in London* (1889), a survey investigating poverty in the city by a team of researchers. Through the mapping of statistics, they revealed that thirty-five percent of the inhabitants of the East End were living in "abject poverty." A second volume succeeded it in 1891, expanding the survey; and Booth's scientific research of London continued until it reached seventeen volumes in 1902–1903.

*Hull-House Maps and Papers* had an extraordinary influence upon the new discipline of sociology at the University of Chicago. It provided the dominant issues and methods that would occupy Chicago sociologists for the next half century. The book illustrated in graphic form the social disorganization resulting from industrialization, and analyzed its effects upon immigrants' daily lives. All the first generation of sociologists at the University of Chicago took an interest in Hull-House's use of mapping to show patterns of social groups, and in its account of the lack of cohesion and order in the rapidly-growing city.

Yet unlike university sociologists, Hull-House women rejected the conception of treating their neighbors—or the city—as a "laboratory for research." Putting the needs of the neighborhood first and viewing families as participants, not objects, they regarded extensive data collecting and statistics as a response to "demands of the community" rather than an "academic discipline." And they stressed crippling economic conditions as a direct cause of the social problems calling for reform, particularly those related to women and children.

As Addams described it in the Preface to *Hull-House Maps and Papers*: the studies were placed before the public as "recorded observations" that were "immediate" and the "result of long acquaintance" with the life of the community. The energies of residents, she explained, "have been chiefly directed, not towards sociological investigation, but to constructive work." That is, the charts, maps, and essays were meant "to present conditions rather than to advance theories," with "the hope of stimulating inquiry and action."

Introductory comments by resident Agnes Holbrook specified that "not only was each house, tenement, and room visited and inspected, but in many cases the reports obtained from one person were borne out by many others." The largest of the eighteen immigrant groups was the Italian one (colored blue on the map of nationalities), followed by Russian and Polish Jews (red and red-striped respectively), and by Bohemians (yellow). Although fewer in number, the Irish (green) had "control of the polls." Notable concerning the wage-maps—also color-coded, in this instance by income—was the fact that wife and children worked to supplement a father's inadequate pay, and that nearly all workers, skilled as well as unskilled, faced regular layoffs.

Kelley as State Factories and Workshop Inspector presented two powerful chapters, one on the "Sweating-System" and another on "Wage-Earning Children," the latter co-authored with her assistant, the labor leader Alzina Stevens. The first, compelling in its thorough and detailed knowledge of tenement manufacturing, contained a harrowing picture of work conditions—of dwellings swarming with vermin, of contaminated garments, and of unbearably low wages. In a little over a year of trying to enforce the hard-won Factory Act of 1893, Kelley judged the legislation ineffective in protecting either exploited garment workers or the unsuspecting public. At best, she felt that the bill could function as a "transition measure, paving the way for the abolition of tenement-house manufacture."

In other branches of industry, she stated, "steam, electricity, and human ingenuity have been pressed into service for the purpose of *organization and centralization*; but in the sweating system this process has been reversed and the division of labor made a means of demoralization, disorganization, and degradation ..." Besides children of all ages in sweatshops, child labor in the Hull-House district ranged from girls and boys working ten-hour shifts as "cash carriers" in retail stores, to underage youth subject to nicotine poisoning in the tobacco industry, young frame-gilders afflicted with stiff fingers and throat disease, and adolescents at risk of mutilation in industries with mechanized equipment.

The Italian colony furnished "a large contingent to the army of bootblacks and newsboys"—lads leaving home "at 2:30 a.m. to secure the first edition of the morning paper, selling each edition as it appears, and filling the intervals with blacking boots and tossing pennies." Then in the winter months, "they gather in the Polk Street

Night-School to doze in the warmth, or torture the teacher with the gamin tricks acquired by day." According to Kelley, "the enforcement of school attendance to the age of sixteen" provided the only solution—the key to child-labor—with state funds for the support of children kept out of school by poverty.

Julia Lathrop, writing about "Cook County Charities," posed the question of "what provision is made to meet sickness, accident, non-employment, old age, and that inevitable accident, death," when private charities and neighborly help have been exhausted? It was at that time, she said, that the Cook County infirmary and mental asylum—which together formed the poorhouse—stood as a last resort. She proceeded to outline the deficiencies of each institution, giving special attention to the political turnover of attendants and the lack of training for nurses. Without a merit system of hiring, she held that Cook County Charities could "never properly perform their duties." And in her estimation, it was up to an informed and vigilant public to use the ballot to demand the good service needed by thousands of dependent people.

Ellen Gates Starr, more than any other Hull-House resident, was responsible for bringing art history and art exhibits to the settlement, for introducing pictures and art appreciation into the Chicago schools, and for perpetuating art as a "living force" in an ugly environment. In her article "Art and Labor," she quoted an English advocate for the arts as maintaining that: "the decision as to whether art should be used in education is, to modern communities, a decision as to whether the mass of the people shall be barbarian or civilized." In her own view, art was an expression of the common life of a people, not of a few unique artists set apart from it. She found hope for artistic creativity in a future state where—unlike the present commercial one with workers subject to the wage law—the "cruel contrasts of surfeit and want, of idleness and overwork" would be eliminated.

Jane Addams' offering to *Hull-House Maps and Papers*—an essay entitled "The Settlement as a Factor in the Labor Movement"— attempted to explain the plight of labor to the middle and affluent classes. She depicted workers caught in a system of dwindling wages, long hours, and unsafe working conditions. Her aim was to show that by uniting to form unions to increase their bargaining power, labor was acting as a counterpart to managers' organizing to influence Washington on their behalf. For Addams, it was critical to ask: "With what attitude stand ye toward the present industrial system?" In other words, do working people have the right to seek a share in the rewards of industry?

Yet she opposed class warfare and the "negative power of conflict," where each side proclaimed itself right and the other side wrong, leaving the outcome to be determined by force. Instead, she placed her hope in the larger vision of solidarity between employees and employers for the "common good." She'd been inspired in Chicago by the sympathy strikes of the unions of "Russian-Jewish cloakmakers, German [printsetters], and Bohemian and Polish butchers" with the railway workers in the 1894 Pullman Strike; and foresaw a growing "social consciousness" that would transcend class lines. It was the settlement's function, she believed, to foster a sense of community to promote "what might be best for society as a whole."

Three sections of the book discussed the Italian, the Jewish, and the Bohemian immigrant populations surrounding Hull-House. The first characterized the Italian colony as impoverished peasants from southern Italy, who left their native land with every intention of returning. "Tillers of the soil" traditionally, but unskilled laborers in Chicago, they could prosper only—according to their Italian interpreter Mastro-Valerio—if resettled in agricultural areas of the country. In the city, they endured harsh-working conditions and a wretched living-environment.

In contrast, the Czech Humpal-Zeman distinguished the Bohemian people of Chicago as conservative artisans struggling to put a little aside from their low wages to invest in a cheap lot, house, and garden. With their love of social life, they found pleasure in excursions to the countryside, festive holidays, and a variety of Bohemian societies and organizations. The women had the reputation of being good housekeepers and cooks, while the men were known to base their political affiliation on their nationality. With regard to the Jewish ghetto, University of Chicago sociologist Charles Zeublin drew a positive picture of the community as family-oriented, centered around the synagogue, and committed to education. He praised the vitality of the Jewish people and their charitable agencies, but found their communal life to be eroded by poverty, bad housing, and an oppressive work situation.

A crucial document of the Progressive Era and the first American study of its kind, *Hull-House Maps and Papers* was a co-operative achievement of women social scientists operating through the settlement movement. The book's statistical data on the wage labor of immigrants—graphically illustrated—redefined poverty by placing blame on the economic system rather than the work spirit of individuals. Addams' position in favor of labor unions appeared radical for the time—as did Hull-House's promotion of government intervention to relieve the misery of sweatshops and slums, and the devastation of recurring economic depression.

Male sociologists, for their part, were engaged in establishing university departments intended to be theoretical and value neutral. At Chicago, a transformation took place in sociology from the mid-1890s through the first decades of the twentieth century— from a discipline that encompassed reform, to one that focused upon science and objectivity. Contributing to such a change was the need for men who filled university positions to fit into the politically restrictive boundaries of higher learning, where significant funding came from prosperous businessmen who sat on Boards of Trustees.

Zeublin, who wrote a chapter for *Hull-House Maps and Papers,* spoke out as a critic of the treatment of workers and had his career as a professor of sociology in the extension division at Chicago terminated. In other institutions of learning as well, social science professors were subject to censure, dismissal, or made to renounce controversial views. Economist Richard Ely, for example, had to submit to a "trial" at the University of Wisconsin in 1894 after "making remarks about the right to strike that offended a regent." It was a dozen years before he returned to labor reform as a founder of the American Association for Labor Legislation in 1906, advocating "the role of the neutral expert."

In comparison, due to its independent financing, Hull-House could better withstand politically and economically motivated attacks against it—enabling residents to pursue pressing problems and follow up with reform activities. The greater portion of the settlement's funding was provided by three wealthy women: the Chicago civic leader Louise de Koven Bowen, Addams' devoted friend Mary Rozet Smith, and businesswoman-philanthropist Helen Culver. As the owner of Hull-House, Culver first rented, then leased, and finally gave the mansion to the settlement, along with adjacent property; however she insisted upon its incorporation. Trustees of the broadly-based corporation largely allowed Addams to set Hull-House's agenda.

Where residents had no professional or independent income, a fellowship system was introduced. That is, upon the detection of a need in the community and the discovery of a person capable of fulfilling it, Addams called upon a rich individual donor to cover the person's salary—as she did with Florence Kelley's first job of operating a labor bureau. Teaching was undertaken by residents and by volunteer lecturers, cutting "the running expenses of the settlement proper to a minimum," Addams explained, while larger sums were "constantly defrayed by generous friends of the House." Her own income came primarily from speaking-tours and writing.

Although overtures were made, Addams declined to integrate the settlement with the University of Chicago. She preferred instructing students and adults "who could not otherwise enter the Academy because of their lack of credentials or funds." Moreover she stood against "academic sociology, elitism, patriarchy, and intellectualism"—all of which became entrenched at Chicago. According to University educator John Dewey—Addams' close friend—Hull-House was an embodiment of his educational belief in "learning by doing." According to Julia Lathrop, what Addams and Hull-House achieved that was new was that they succeeded in weaving "human sympathy with the scientific method."

## *Sources*

Bremner, Robert H., ed. *Children and Youth in America: A Documentary History*. Cambridge: Harvard University Press, 1971, 612.

Deegan, Mary Jo. *Jane Addams and the Men of the Chicago School, 1892–1918.* New Brunswick, NJ: Transaction Publishers, 1990, 2, 6, 34–40, 49–51, and chapter 3.

Kelly, Florence. *The Selected Letters of Florence Kelley, 1869–1931.* Edited by Kathryn Sklar and Beverly Wilson Palmer. Urbana: University of Illinois Press, 2009, xxx, 49.

Knight, Louise W. *Jane Addams: Spirit in Action*. NY: Norton & Company, 2010, 82–83, 92–3, 105.

Menand, Louis. *The Metaphysical Club*. New York: Farrar, Straus, and Giroux, 2001, chapter 12.

Muncy, Robyn. *Creating a Female Dominion in American Reform*. NY: Oxford University Press, 1991, 17–18.

Residents of Hull-House. *Hull-House Maps and Papers*. Introduction by Rima Lunin Schultz. Urbana: University of Illinois Press, 2006, vii–viii, 3–76, 91–204.

# CHAPTER 7

# Alice Hamilton

I n her autobiography *Exploring the Dangerous Trades,* Alice Hamilton looks back upon an eventful life as a pioneer in industrial medicine; while in her personal letters, she expresses her thoughts and feelings at particular points of time. Both convey a determination to carve out a professional role for herself in a new and challenging field. However, in her words: "I should never have taken up the cause of the working class had I not lived at Hull-House and learned much from Jane Addams, Florence Kelley, Julia Lathrop, and others."

Until she left home to enter a private school at age seventeen, Hamilton led a sheltered existence among family and relatives in Fort Wayne, Indiana. Her grandfather, a native of Northern Ireland, had arrived in the frontier town in 1828, built up a fortune, and become one of the community's leading citizens. Three generations of Hamiltons lived in elegant homes on the extensive holdings of real estate he'd acquired; and eight of his eleven Fort Wayne grand-children—including Alice—formed a tightly-knit group of cousins.

The family valued education and intellectual accomplishments over wealth and social standing. Hamilton boys were sent East to college, and girls to Miss Porter's finishing school in Farmington, Connecticut. Except for attending church services and teaching Sunday school at the Presbyterian Church, the cousins rarely mingled with "outsiders." As children they played together, inventing lively games like Robin Hood and the Siege of Troy; and as adolescents they gathered in the evening to entertain themselves with word games and musical activities. The deep friendships they formed endured, most notably Alice's with Agnes, her confidant to whom she wrote many of the letters selected to be published posthumously.

Alice and her three sisters—all born within six years—were home-schooled, mainly in languages and literature and history. Their father taught them Latin and encouraged them to read widely and use the *Encyclopedia Britannica* and other reference sources from his library. He had a "passion for theology," and as an initial project assigned Alice to try to find "proof of the doctrine of the Trinity in the Bible," a book she grew to know well. Their mother, who'd spent the Civil War years in Europe, saw to it that they learned to speak French, and she read aloud such English novels as George Eliot's *Mill on the Floss* and *Adam Bede* with them. She wanted her daughters to pursue their own interests rather than be sacrificed to the "family claim," as a number of the cousins had been. It was from her mother, Alice said, that she realized "personal liberty was the most precious thing in life."

Of the four girls, Edith—the eldest—studied classics at Bryn Mawr College and in Germany, became headmistress of the Bryn Mawr Preparatory School, and later wrote the highly successful books *The Greek Way* and *Mythology*. The third daughter Margaret (Alice was the second) graduated in science from Bryn Mawr, went on to study abroad, and then taught at the college's preparatory school. Norah, the youngest of the four, was an artist trained at the Art Student's League in New York and in Europe, who also worked as a teacher for disadvantaged children. A brother, the fifth and much younger child—nicknamed Quint—earned an advanced degree in Romance languages at Johns Hopkins College and became a professor at the University of Illinois. Only Quint married.

Due to the failure of their father's wholesale grocery business in the mid-1880s, and to economic downturns in the 1890s, the family suffered financial difficulties and had to sell off inherited property. Both Edith and Alice as the eldest daughters realized it would be up to them to be self-supporting, if they were to experience the full and meaningful lives they aspired to. Of the possibilities open to women, Edith decided upon teaching and Alice chose medicine. As she related in her autobiography, the decision was made not because she was scientifically-minded, but "because as a doctor I could go anywhere I pleased—to far-off lands or to city slums—and be quite sure that I could be of use anywhere."

After making up for her deficiencies in science, she entered the University of Michigan's medical program as a special student. As it happened, she received one of the finest educations in medicine in the country, with solid scientific training in the laboratory—along with her "first taste of emancipation." The impressive, youthful faculty was committed to research in the German tradition in such basic fields as biochemistry, bacteriology, physiology, and pharmacology; and her clinical work involved the microscope and chemical analysis, as well as physical examinations and diagnoses. One-third of her graduating class in 1893 were women, in a school that had been receptive to female students for some twenty years.

In keeping with the scientific foundation she obtained at Michigan, she turned to bacteriology and pathology as a career instead of the usual practice of medicine. However advised to spend time in a hospital to complete her training, she worked as an intern at the New England Hospital for Women and Children in Boston— where she especially enjoyed being on call at the dispensary as each case meant a new adventure, often in immigrant and black neighborhoods.

Summers brought her to the family retreat at Mackinac Island in Upper Michigan, "a beautiful island, lying in the Straits, with Lake Huron to the east and Lake Michigan to the west, their horizons as wide as the ocean." All the sisters loved Mackinac "passionately, almost painfully." As described by Alice, "Its woods included white birch and silver birch, beech, hemlock, and those pines which one sees only in the North..." She recalled nights in an open boat with "no sound but the lapping of the water in that vast solemn night, or now and then the loon's long cry, so musical and so deeply mournful."

The two older girls embarked on a year of graduate study in Germany in 1895. While women weren't admitted to German universities, they could attend lecture classes with a professor's permission. At Leipzig and in Munich, Alice discovered her lot to be easier than her sister's "because I wanted laboratory work, which nobody objected to." Rigorous work rather than long hours prevailed in the sciences, yet it impressed her that the Germans "produced more first-class scientific studies than did the hard-working Americans I knew at home." Despite her exasperation at the German treatment of women as inferior—it was "a man's world"—she had positive feelings about "the warmth and kindliness of the people and the easy, simple way they took the enjoyable things in life," like music and getting out in the countryside. Even in the labs, there could be gaiety—and at scientific meetings, a refreshing informality.

Returning to the United States she continued her graduate study, this time at Johns Hopkins' Medical School during its "great years," then accepted a position in Chicago as professor of pathology at the Woman's Medical School of Northwestern University. This enabled her to realize her dream to live at Hull-House. She later held that "the life there satisfied every longing, for companionship, for the excitement of new experiences, for constant intellectual stimulation, and for the sense of being caught up in a big movement which enlisted my enthusiastic loyalty." She remained a resident for twenty-two years, from age twenty-eight to fifty, and afterwards returned for several months each year while Addams was alive.

Still, in the beginning it proved difficult to do three things at once—her job, social service, and scientific research. It was her experience at Hull-House, though, that alerted her to the problem of industrial disease, which would be her life's work. Initially she operated a well-baby clinic, probed cocaine traffic by druggists to schoolboys, and investigated the source of a city-wide typhoid epidemic. When Northwestern closed its medical school for women, she became a bacteriologist at the new Memorial Institute for Infectious Diseases in Chicago, one of the first creative research centers of its kind in the country.

During her early years at Hull-House, she derived pleasure from the neighborhood children she came in contact with at the settlement. On several occasions she "took as many as thirty Italian youngsters on a weekend expedition . . . With cries of 'Doctor Hammel,' they trooped down the street after her and vied for her attention." And she formed a special relationship with Florence Kelley's teen-age son Ko, who often accompanied her and a few other residents enthusiastic about the new sport of cycling, making regular Sunday trips out of the city.

In 1908, a decade after arriving in Chicago, her career changed decisively with her appointment by the governor to the Illinois Commission on Occupational Diseases. Put in charge of a study on lead poisoning in 1910, she found evidence of extensive use of lead in Illinois industries, at a time when sick workers were fired without recourse or compensation. In its acute form, victims suffered convulsions, paralysis, and mental decline. Hamilton described four histories of stricken men in her autobiography. In one typical example:

> A Hungarian, thirty-six years old, worked for seven years grinding lead paint. During this time he had three attacks of colic, with vomiting and headaches. I saw him in the hospital, a skeleton of a man, looking almost twice his age, his limbs soft and flabby, his muscles wasted . . . He lay in an apathetic condition, rousing when spoken to and answering rationally, but slowly, with often an appreciable delay, then sinking back into apathy.

Her report documented 578 instances of lead poisoning, and resulted in the state's passing an occupational disease law to protect employees exposed to hazardous work conditions. Subsequently the United States Bureau of Labor asked her to conduct a similar investigation on the federal level; and she started with a study of the white-lead industries responsible for lead dust. It was up to her to locate and gain entry to suspected factories, then track down cases to determine the incidence of poison in a given plant. Increasingly this was done by consulting the records of hospitals and dispensaries, and by visiting sick workers at home where they could talk freely.

In an era when the federal government lacked the power to implement a law, she took it upon herself to apply personal persuasion to those in charge. And she succeeded to a surprising degree. "A woman of breeding and exquisite appearance," in the words of her friend the Harvard law professor Felix Frankfurter, she prepared herself thoroughly for each inspection and was "disarmingly sincere and forthright about her findings." By recommending safety measures such as respirators, exhaust and sprinkling systems, and regular medical exams, she sought to save immigrant workers from having to choose between risking their health and unemployment.

Unlike in Europe, where industrial diseases were treated with the utmost concern by medical specialists and led to government controls and worker compensation, American physicians downplayed such a solution as "tainted with socialism or with feminine sentimentality for the poor." Yet by her own account: "One would find it difficult to point to any disease equally prevalent, equally serious, equally controllable, which has been so neglected by the medical profession in America as industrial lead-poisoning." Disastrous for the working class, second only to tuberculosis in its devastation, lead was "as endemic to industrial districts as malaria was to the swamps."

Her articles on lead poisoning for scientific journals presented statistics to demonstrate the contrast "between lead work in the United States under conditions of neglect and ignorance, and comparable work in England and Germany, under intelligent control." For example, on a visit to England in 1910, she discovered that "a factory which produced white and red lead, employing ninety men, had not had a case of lead poisoning in five successive years," whereas in an American plant with eighty-five men, medical records showed "thirty-five men 'leaded' in six months." She accounted for the difference by England's effective inspection system.

Hamilton's employment by the Labor Department, which lasted until 1920, allowed her to break the bounds set for women of her class and generation. It also gave her an opportunity to travel extensively—from the white lead factories of the East Coast and Pennsylvania, to the lead smelters of Illinois, Missouri, and Nebraska; the mines and smelters of the Rocky Mountain states; and the copper camps of Arizona. Sent to Arizona to study the effect of vibrations of the jackhammer upon workers, she experienced the exploration of a mine for the first time. To quote her account of the descent eight-hundred feet below:

> Dressed in miner's overalls and helmet, the latter with a safety lamp fastened in front, we stepped into a "cage," which is a flimsy, shaky elevator, devoid of walls or anything else one can cling to, and dropped down into darkness . . . In the mine I was expected to follow my leader . . . So I trudged along, stooping to avoid overhangs, and thankful for the protection my helmet provided against bumps, scrambling on hands and knees up into a stope [excavation] to see the hammer at work . . .

With American participation in the First World War, she was called upon to investigate the manufacture of explosives, chiefly TNT in munitions plants. She identified some twenty-four hundred poisoned workers, among more than thirty-thousand men exposed to a variety of toxic substances. Her unconventional career stood out even from the fields her Hull-House colleagues carved out, which centered upon women and children. In 1919, in recognition of her unique achievements, Harvard appointed her assistant professor of industrial medicine—the first female faculty member in the Harvard Medical School's history. She went on to teach for fifteen years in the school's program of industrial hygiene, a forerunner in the discipline. According to terms she negotiated, her courses took place during the fall semester, leaving the spring one free for her own work and a return to Hull-House.

Altogether her active professional life spanned over five decades. As she expressed it—it covered "the period of passionate and hopeful idealism in the nineties; of slowly increasing disillusion culminating in the shock of war in 1914; of the war years with their intolerance and bitterness and wave of reaction; of the 'giddy twenties' when, underneath the surface froth, I saw unemployment and exploitation; [and of] the soberer thirties with the increasing movement toward social justice."

## Sources

Hamilton, Alice. *Exploring the Dangerous Trades*. Boston: Little, Brown and Company, 1943, 3–17, 25–37, 117–126, 197–198, and chapters 3, 4, 9.

Sicherman, Barbara. *Alice Hamilton: A Life in Letters*. Cambridge: Harvard University Press, 1984, 1–6, 33–36, 90–91, 118–120, 232–233.

# CHAPTER 8

# The Progressive Era

The Progressive Era extended from the mid-1890s until America entered World War I—or according to another view, from the start of the twentieth century until 1920. During these two decades, social reformers increasingly turned to legislative action to combat industrial and urban ills. Government was regarded by progressives as a means for furthering democracy and the public welfare, as well as defending individual liberties. Hull-House as a settlement helped transform the traditional way of assisting the poor through charity, into a responsibility of government to protect women and children exploited in an age of unregulated capitalism. Or, as Jane Addams characterized it, the settlements "turned a generation of young Americans from philanthropists to reformers."

In her first of eleven books—*Democracy and Social Ethics* (1902)—Addams presented a sympathetic interpretation of impoverished workers to her middle-class readers. It was an account that Supreme Court Judge Oliver Wendell Holmes credited with giving him "insight into the point of view of the working man and the poor;" and the philosopher William James called "one of the great books of our time." In it, she explained how workers represented a culture of their own, one alien to that of the middle class. The method she used was to compare the charity visitor's values with those of her clients in need—the former, "bourgeois habits of temperance and thrift;" the latter, an opposing set of responses.

For instance, in Addams' words: "A most striking incongruity, at once apparent, is the difference between the emotional kindness with which relief is given by one poor neighbor to another poor neighbor, and the guarded care with which relief is given by a charity visitor to a charity recipient." To illustrate, she drew upon the "practice of *saving,* which seems quite commendable in a comfortable part of town," but appears "almost criminal in a poorer quarter where the next-door neighbor needs food."

Moreover the charity visitor's conception of the "horrors of the neighborhood saloon" might not be shared by the family bread-earner, "who remembers all the kindnesses he has received there." As his club and social center, it hosted "free lunch and treating" when he was "out of work and not able to pay up, and a loan . . . when charity help was miles away and he was threatened with eviction." Addams also differentiated the values of "girls of social standing" from those of "poor working girls," concerning clothes. The latter spent a disproportionate share of their wages on clothing, feeling that that was how they were judged.

Thus girls' clubs which provided evening activities fared best down-town, where young wage-earners from the tenements and young ladies of means could meet in neutral territory; and their clothes "superficially looked alike." The charity agent herself disapproved of spending too much and focusing too heavily on "appearances." Yet she came to realize it was largely due to the disparity in education and the gap in living conditions of the two classes, while "street clothes and manners" could readily be imitated.

In an age when poverty was considered "synonymous with vice and laziness," and the prosperous man was thought to be "the righteous man," charity involved intrusive investigations to determine the worthy and the unworthy poor. The sheer desperation of the Depression of 1893 brought about co-operation between charities and settlements in Chicago, although they remained divided on the issue of reform. Not until Addams was elected president of the National Conference of Charities and Correction in 1909 (it became the National Conference of Social Work in 1917) did the emphasis of the organization change "from correction to prevention, and from charity to social reform."

*The Spirit of Youth and the City Streets*—Addams' third book (1909)—again addressed the adverse effect of the industrial city upon its inhabitants, this time upon its youth and especially upon their "play." The Greeks of the classical period had cultivated play "with careful solicitude, building the theater and stadium as they built the market place and the temple;" while in the medieval age, "knights held their tourneys, the guilds their pageants, the people their dances, and the church its festivals." The modern city alone was failing in its responsibility to furnish recreation for its youth—failing to organize their play at a time when factories controlled their work.

Such a failure meant that satisfying the youthful desire for pleasure fell to business, whose main purpose was profit. Just as industrial enterprises exploited the labor of the young, so, too, tawdry dance halls with alcohol ever-present consumed their meager wages. Overworked girls seeking gaiety and romance, bored boys out for adventure and a thrill ended up in the hands of unscrupulous entrepreneurs eager for financial gain at their expense. Commercialized "entertainment" replaced community-based activities, deepening the rift between the immigrant populations that had flocked to the factories, and their American-born, city-bred children.

Perhaps Hull-House's most significant contribution to its immigrant neighbors lay in helping them preserve their native customs and traditions. To ease their Americanization and, in turn, introduce Americans to the immigrants' diverse cultures and heritage, the settlement celebrated their festivals, exhibited their art and handicrafts, performed their music, and produced their native plays. Grace Abbott, Hull-House resident and, from 1908 to 1917, director of the newly-created Immigrants' Protective League, even traveled to the homeland of recent arrivals from southeastern Europe. Wanting to understand the "immigrant problem" at its source, she visited Hungary, Croatia, and Galicia—and would have gone on to Bulgaria and Greece, except for warlike conditions in the Balkans.

Meeting in the "old country" with the families of her Hull-House neighbors, Abbott learned first-hand about savings lost in immigrant banks, women whose husbands remarried in America, men coming back ill or injured, and skilled workers forced to take menial jobs in Chicago. Upon her return, Abbott resumed her efforts on behalf of down-trodden immigrants—the "forgotten men" (and women) of those days. Her aim was to bring justice to vulnerable members of society, assist them in adjusting to industrial life, and provide for their basic needs. Moreover she turned out to be uniquely qualified as an administrator.

She had what lawyers call "a good legal mind," and claimed to be "born with an interest in law and politics." A student of administrative law under a recognized authority of the time—the legal scholar Ernst Freund at the University of Chicago—she was able to see for herself in her capacity as head of the Protective League if social legislation could be enforced in the way it was intended. As her sister Edith later remarked, the three great leaders of social reform in America—Jane Addams, Julia Lathrop, and Florence Kelley—each considered Grace as "the shining light among the younger generation of social workers."

Abbott's nine years with the Immigrants' Protective League opened with a struggle against employment agencies that over-charged for their service, often without securing jobs or else dispatching laborers out of the city. Thus a contingent of Bulgarians was sent at its own expense to Arkansas, and Poles to Wyoming, for largely non-existent or temporary employment. Both had to walk back to Chicago. At Abbott's instigation and with the assistance of Freund, a state law was drafted—and passed in 1909—for the regulation of employment agencies.

An investigation into the safeguarding of immigrant savings followed, in a day when private banking in Illinois lacked controls. Given, too, that the court system had no competent interpreters, the league advocated for both public defenders and ethnic translators. It was not uncommon for immigrants to be confined to prison merely on account of poverty. The 1920 census recorded almost three hundred thousand Americans imprisoned in a single year for non-payment of fines.

From the very start, the league defended newcomers from "porters, ticket agents, and cabbies" prepared to take advantage of them. And in an article for the old *Chicago Evening Post*, Abbott dealt with the problem of "lost immigrant girls" from eastern Europe. Although put on proper trains by federal inspectors at Ellis Island, a fair number never met up with those awaiting them in Chicago. For whatever the reason, no connection was made, either at the railroad station or a private address. As a response, the league obtained the names of girls traveling alone, arranged for train supervision, and reserved a waiting room at the terminal where ethnic speakers could help them locate relatives or secure lodging.

The issue of immigration restriction grew steadily more controversial during the Progressive Era, especially of southeastern Europeans as distinct from those of an earlier period from northern and western Europe. In 1912, Abbott appeared before a congressional committee to speak against a required literacy test—testimony reported to have persuaded President Taft to veto the literacy bill approved by Congress. As one settlement house leader commented, "The ability to read and write is what we can most easily give the immigrants when they arrive." Abbott's own immigration plan focused on the federal government's supplying advice and help, rather than stressing restriction and deportation.

As she put it:

> A great means of enriching our national life is lost if
> we give to those who are coming from the various nations
> of Europe the impression that we desire to neglect all but
> the Anglo-Saxon element in our population.

By the presidential election of 1912, most settlement workers favored national immigrant legislation; and at their insistence, a statement "to promote the assimilation, education, and advancement of immigrants" was included in Theodore Roosevelt's Progressive Party platform.

⸺⸱ ⸱⸺

Hull-House's dedication to improving the lot of immigrants extended to blacks as well. Both Jane Addams and Florence Kelley were founding members of the National Association for the Advancement of Colored People (NAACP) in 1909, and served on its interracial Board of Directors with W. E. B. DuBois, the dominant black civil rights activist of the period. He later wrote: "As a Board member, Kelley came regularly to meetings . . . and she asked questions . . . pointed, penetrating, devastating questions . . . Save for Jane Addams, there is not another social worker in the United States who has had either her insight or her daring so far as the American Negro is concerned."

It was Addams and Kelley as co-editors of *Hull-House Maps and Papers* that became "facilitators and role models" for DuBois' *The Philadelphia Negro*—the first documented investigation into the conditions of a black community. Eminently equipped to conduct such an investigation, DuBois at twenty-eight possessed the first PhD from Harvard of an African-American and two years of post-graduate study in Germany in the rising field of social science. Appointed instructor of sociology at the University of Pennsylvania during the Philadelphia project (from 1896–1898), he looked forward to applying the methods of scientific research to the Negro's situation.

But his hopes for a professional life at the college went unfulfilled, and he lived in an atmosphere of "poverty and crime" at a black settlement annex. As he reported it: "Murder sat on our doorsteps, police were our government, and philanthropy dropped in with periodic advice." Nevertheless his thoroughgoing, perceptive study of the largest and oldest Negro community in the North—from the point of view of environment rather than race—received praise from reviewers at its publication in 1899. Although he never succeeded in being accepted by white, male sociologists, he had a productive relationship with female reformers associated with

Hull-House—as was the case with Isabel Eaton who undertook the section on domestic labor for the Philadelphia study.

As the most prominent voice in favor of settlements working in the community for social change, Addams shared DuBois' commitment to eliminating racism. However the problem of inequality and discrimination continued to fester. In 1896, the Supreme Court sanctioned the "separate but equal" doctrine for black and white citizens; by 1900, the Negro had been effectively disenfranchised in the South; and during the 1890s, more than two thousand Americans were lynched, the great majority of them men of African descent. In Chicago, the black journalist Ida Wells Barnett, a friend of Addams, devoted herself to a lifelong crusade against lynching—a subject fraught with racial hysteria.

Early in the new century (1903), Hull-House reformers participated in the founding of the National Women's Trade Union League, which sought to organize female workers to secure better working conditions. Male labor leaders co-operated; however the initiative came from the settlements and those associated with them—including Addams, Kelley, and fiery young Chicagoan Mary Kenney, a "bookbinder by trade, but an agitator and organizer by temperament." Backed by an impressive alliance of women that crossed class lines, the Trade Union League united workers, settlement reformers, and members of the middle and upper class sympathetic to labor.

According to Addams, she and others had joined the league to stand in solidarity with the union women, "to share their blunders with them as well as their successes." She understood how unrealistic it was "to support only those movements that made no mistakes." In the city-wide garment strike of Chicago in 1910–11, Ellen Gates Starr entered the picket lines, Addams raised relief funds and pressed for mediation, while Grace Abbott both picketed and sought public support for the strikers. As Alice Hamilton recalled: "At Hull-House one got into the labor movement as a matter of course, without realizing how or when." Starr, who felt strongly about labor rights, became a socialist in 1916—and a Catholic in 1920.

Julia Lathrop, for her part, had spoken out to social workers in the early 1890s about the future of labor, with her usual foresight:

> Hull-House is profoundly interested in the labor movement . . . Several unions of women have been organized at the settlement and in several cases it has been possible to exert a conciliatory influence in strikes. The trade-union must be reckoned with as a fact . . . I do not know what modifications of our present economic and industrial life are to grow out of the labor movement, but of this I feel certain, that if the movement fails to develop reasonably it is the fault not more of those who direct it than of those who stand aloof from it.

Henry Demarest Lloyd—Hull-House supporter and the author of *Wealth Against Commonwealth* (1894 critique of industrial capitalism) and *Strike of Millionaires Against Miners* (1890 story of Spring Valley, Illinois)—became convinced that the alternative to labor reform was revolution, that "we must either get redress for these 'wrongs' through the state or through anarchy." As such, he made it a lifetime endeavor to inform his countrymen of existing conditions for workers. While his political position was much like Kelley's, he had no network of men's organizations behind him like female reformers had built up with women's groups.

During the 1890s, despite the enactment of the Sherman Antitrust Act, its weak enforcement by the courts meant that corporations often remained without accountability. In 1910, steelworkers continued to labor twelve-hours a day, while "twenty-percent of the work force were still subject to a seven-day week." All that time, industrial accidents took a frightful toll on human life; and periodic downturns, seasonal layoffs, and general job and wage instability provoked widespread misery and unrest.

—3 ᴇ—

The General Federation of Women's Clubs, a voluntary association established in 1890, grew out of earlier nineteenth-century literary societies that gradually expanded their activities to include a variety of reforms for the benefit of women and children. Child labor was a major concern. "Mothers pensions" for impoverished widows was another. And together with Julia Lathrop, the Chicago club succeeded in enacting a juvenile court in 1899, which served as a model for other states. Women's clubs paved the way, also, in campaigning for compulsory school attendance, in creating the country's public libraries, and in gaining passage of the Pure Food and Drug Act. While black women were excluded from the General Federation, they set up associations of their own to respond to injustice.

The decades of struggle for reform reached a climax with the Progressive Party candidacy of Theodore Roosevelt in the presidential election of 1912. The Progressive platform encompassed measures that settlement and social workers had advocated for twenty years—and drafted at their convention that very spring as "minimum social standards for industry." Notable among them were the eight-hour work day, the abolition of sweatshops, prohibition of child labor, regulation of employment for women, and a system of accident and unemployment insurance—along with woman's suffrage. At the Progressive Convention in Chicago, overflowing with women supporters, enthusiastic applause greeted Jane Addams' seconding of Roosevelt's nomination. "Not even the Colonel [Roosevelt himself] got much more rousing cheers . . ."

Above all, it was the Progressive Party program which mattered most to reformers—that is, its social and industrial planks. As Addams declared: "The platform contains all the things I have been fighting for, for more than a decade." However she still struggled to come to terms with its inclusion of building two battleships a year, and all but left the convention when it refused to seat Negro delegates from the South.

Settlement workers threw themselves into the Progressive cause, with no one surpassing Addams in her efforts on its behalf. "The most famous woman in America" in 1912, she was much sought-after as a campaign speaker; and her appearances attracted record crowds. An election day win by the Democratic nominee Woodrow Wilson was not a complete surprise. Yet progressives were convinced that they'd made an important first step, that victory would be theirs, that a new political era was dawning. As it turned out, such prospects did not come to pass. Not only were there discouraging setbacks, but World War I erupted in Europe to cast a black cloud over reform.

## Sources

Abbott, Edith. "The Hull-House of Jane Addams." *Social Service Review*, September 1952.

———"A Sister's Memories." *Social Service Review*, vol. 13. Chicago: University of Chicago, Sept.1939, 351-408.

Addams, Jane. *The Social Thought of Jane Addams*. Edited by Christopher Lasch. Indianapolis: Bobbs-Merrill Company, 1965, 162–174.

Costin, Lela B. *Two Sisters for Social Justice: A Biography of Grace and Edith Abbott*. Urbana: University of Illinois Press, 1983, chapters 4 and 8.

Davis, Allen F. *Spearheads for Reform*. NY: Oxford University Press, 1967, 92–94, 194–205.

Deegan, Mary Jo. "DuBois and the Hull-House Women: 1895–1899." *American Sociologist*, Winter 1988.

DuBois, W. E. B. *The Philadelphia Negro*, 1899. Ebook and Tests Archive, Universal Library: https://archive.org/details/universallibrary (accessed 2007).

Flexner, Eleanor and Ellen Fitzpatrick. *Century of Struggle*. Cambridge: Harvard University Press, 1996, 171–172.

Goodwin, Doris Kearns. *The Bully Pulpit: Theodore Roosevelt, William Howard Taft, and the Golden Age of Journalism*. NY: Simon and Schuster, 2013, 37–49, 678–690.

Hamington, Maurice. *The Social Philosophy of Jane Addams*. Urbana: University of Illinois Press, 2009, 109–125.

Knight, Louise W. *Jane Addams: Spirit in Action*. NY: Norton, 2010, 104–109, 131–135.

Morris, Richard and William Greenleaf. *USA: History of a Nation*, vol. 2. Chicago: Rand McNally, 1969, 441, 468,

Muncy, Robyn. *Creating a Female Dominion in American Reform*. NY: Oxford University Press, 1991, 35.

# CHAPTER 9

# More New Organizations

## I. Florence Kelley and the Consumers League

With the November 1896 defeat of Democratic governor John Altgeld—a pioneer in placing women in Illinois state positions—the new Republican governor terminated Florence Kelley's work as Chief Factory Inspector that following August. The man chosen to replace her had long been on the payroll of the Alton Illinois Glass Company, the number-one employer of children in the state. And he'd been "convicted of violating the very act he was now appointed to enforce." Throughout his term as inspector—as Kelley noted—"there were no violations of law by glass manufacturers prosecuted, nor was the child labor law of Illinois amended."

At Hull-House she had pictured the glass factory's exploitation of underage children so vividly that years later Alice Hamilton could still visualize:

> Little figures drawn from the orphan asylums and put in flatboats and drifted down the river . . . sent into work as "blowers' dogs," working by night or day, at any age they might be. She [Kelley] had . . . seen them on the night shift and she had stood outside at the door and had seen the night shift come out, these little fellows trotting behind the men they worked for and going perfectly naturally into a saloon with them for a pick-me-up before they staggered home to go to bed.

Deprived of a steady income, Kelley looked to find other sources of revenue to support herself and her three children—meaningful work that would utilize her talents and experience. She inquired about a position on a federal commission for industrial reform, pursued another as New York factory inspector, and took stock of academia. But with no results.

It was finally through articles, speeches, and library work that she secured employment. The first involved contributing a series of analyses of the labor scene to a German journal of social legislation and statistics—preparing up-to-date accounts of American factory inspection, social laws, labor statistics, and strikes. The second entailed speaking at conferences and conventions, where she was much in demand.

Evenings she took charge of the periodicals department at the Crerar Reference Library in downtown Chicago, a resource for economics, science, and medicine. Upon her return to the settlement at night, a group of residents would be waiting with hot chocolate in anticipation of hearing anecdotes of her time at the library, or a narration of her adventures as Illinois Factory Inspector. It was with wit, fervor, and rare insight that she re-created her four-year fight against the evils of child labor, sweat-work, and an unlimited workday for women.

From the Consumers League's early years, she assumed a leading role in the movement. Established in New York City in 1891 to exert consumer pressure against the employment of children in industry—and improve the labor conditions of working women—the league soon spread to other cities, including Boston, Philadelphia, and Chicago. In 1899, the local leagues united into a national organization, which Kelley was asked to head as General Secretary. In her new capacity, she brought her skills as Illinois factory inspector to bear upon the production of consumer goods. A special "white label" was designed and a "white list" compiled to identify products that met the league's requirements for fair working standards.

A dynamic director, she traveled extensively—setting up new leagues, launching educational campaigns, delivering speeches, inspecting factories, and attending meetings and conferences. By the end of her fifth year, some sixty-four leagues were active in twenty states. Included among the diverse audiences she addressed, in addition to consumer ones, were social reformers, women's clubs, trade unions, religious gatherings, state legislatures, and congressional committees—along with colleges and universities. Frances Perkins, Secretary of Labor under President Franklin Roosevelt and the first woman to hold a cabinet post, expressed the inspirational effect that Kelley had had upon her as a student at Mount Holyoke, and on others like her:

> She was willing to go into  . . . far corners where a handful of girls were students and tell them about the program which she was evolving for industrial and human and social justice . . . She took a whole group of young people, formless in their aspirations, and molded their aspirations for social justice into a definite purpose, into a program that had meaning and that had experience and that had practicality back of it.

Above all, Kelley wanted workers to share in the benefits of their labor. In America, social policy traditionally had been "initiated more by activists in voluntary associations than by legislators, civil servants, or organized labor." She sought, accordingly, for the Consumers League to promote protective legislation for women by combining the economic clout of consumers with the collective strength of wage-earners. Her book on "ethical gains through legislation," held that workers' rights would come only with "comprehensive statutes sustained by decisions of the highest courts, and enforced by endless effort of purchasers and wage-earners . . ." To Kelley, the rights of laborers encompassed that of a child to an education, and of an adult to time free from work, as well as sufficient pay to cover the cost of living and health.

With Illinois' Supreme Court ruling that labor laws violated a worker's "freedom of contract" under the Fourteenth Amendment, she increasingly favored the use of gender as a means to legitimize social legislation. In a 1908 court case in Oregon—*Muller versus Oregon*—a state law limiting women to a ten-hour workday was upheld on the grounds that it protected the health and safety of its female citizens. And when the case reached the nation's highest court, for the first time—in the "Brandeis brief" named after the defense counsel (and future Supreme Court judge) Louis Brandeis—social, economic, and scientific data rather than abstract arguments and legal precedents were presented to defend a labor law enacted by a state.

Much earlier, in 1891, Brandeis had warned the legislature in his home state of Massachusetts that laws "which failed to take into consideration the conditions for which they were designed" wouldn't be effective. As soon as the Consumers League of Oregon notified Kelley that the Muller case would be decided before the Supreme Court in Washington, she turned to him as "the people's lawyer." He asked her to assemble as many facts as possible related to women's labor, from whatever sources available. His final brief featured two pages of legal issues and over a hundred pages of the detrimental effects of long work hours on the "health, safety, and general welfare of women."

Evidence was drawn from factory inspectors' reports, medical commissions, and records of work hours in Britain, countries in Europe, and a few American states. What stood out—according to Kelley's assistant Josephine Goldmark, the major researcher for the case—were "contrasting pictures of misery and its alleviation . . . of exploited workers under unregulated hours . . . and the regeneration that followed a more decent limitation of hours." In the Supreme Court's majority opinion, recognition was given to the new "sociological" defense that called upon justices to consider the ways their decisions affected "real people's lives."

Most industrial nations did not subject social reform measures enacted by parliament to a constitution based on individual rights—which meant that they were not overturned by a court on constitutional grounds, as in America. However the Tenth Amendment of the *Constitution* did reserve for the states the rights and powers not delegated to the federal government, including the regulation of matters affecting the health and safety of their citizens. Thus as Brandeis understood, state laws regulating work for women could be validated by the country's highest court *if shown to be related to their health and safety.* In upholding hours legislation in Oregon, the court ruling also "confirmed the validity of nineteen other state laws limiting the working day for women in industry," laws that hung on the Oregon decision.

It should be stressed that in furthering workplace laws for women, Kelley intended advances to become an opening "wedge" to protect male wage-earners as well. She employed gender as a strategy in order to extend social rights to *all* workers, rights that other advanced nations championed through class-based labor movements and a Labor Party. And she came to believe that without a minimum wage, legislation restricting work hours and the league's other guarantees would be "of little value"—that "low wages produced more poverty than all other causes together."

Not until 1937 would the Supreme Court reverse course and "accept a minimum wage case as a proper exercise of the state's [protective] power of the Tenth Amendment." To Kelley's colleagues, the decision brought to mind her discerning comment at a social work conference back in 1911, over a quarter of a century earlier in the long struggle to establish the constitutionality of wage laws:

> But is the trouble really in the *Constitution*? Or is it in the judges?

Of Kelley's more than thirty years in charge of the National Consumers League, Felix Frankfurter—another future member of the Supreme Court who served as league counsel—maintained that she had had: "probably the largest single share in shaping the social history of the United States during the first thirty years of the [20th] century . . ."

He went on to say that "hers was no doubt a powerful if not

decisive role in securing legislation for the removal of the most glaring abuses of our hectic industrialization following the Civil War."

## Sources

Blumberg, Dorothy R. *Florence Kelley: the Making of a Social Pioneer,* New York: Augustus Kelley Publishers, 1966, 175–178.

Downey, Kirston. *The Woman Behind the New Deal: The Life of Frances Perkins, FDR's Secretary of Labor and His Moral Conscience.* NY: Doubleday, 2008, 11–13.

Flexner, Eleanor, and Ellen Fitzpatrick. *Century of Struggle: the Woman's Rights Movement in the United States.* Cambridge: Harvard University Press, 1996, 206–207.

Goldmark, Josephine. *Impatient Crusader: Florence Kelley's Life Story.* Urbana: University of Illinois Press, 1953, 47-50, 56-65, 142, chapter 13, and 179.

Kelly, Florence. *The Selected Letters of Florence Kelley, 1869–1931.* Edited by Kathryn Sklar and Beverly Wilson Palmer. Urbana: University of Illinois Press, 2009, 499–500.

Sklar, Kathryn Kish. *Florence Kelley and the Nation's Work.* New Haven: Yale University Press, 1995, 291–299.

*United States Constitution.* Amendment X.

Urofsky, Melvin I. *Louis D. Brandeis: A Life.* New York: Pantheon Books, 2009, 201–227.

*West Coast Hotel Co. v.* Parrish [1937]. *West's Encyclopedia of American Law. 2005.* Encyclopedia.com, (April10, 2015). http://www.encylcopedia.com/doc/162-3437004682.html

## II. Julia Lathrop and the Children's Bureau

The idea for a Children's Bureau in the federal government can be traced to Lillian Wald at the Henry Street Settlement in New York City—Florence Kelley's residence during her years with the Consumers League. Legend has it that one morning in 1903 as the two women were at breakfast opening their mail and reading the newspaper, a letter surfaced asking why nothing had been done about the summer death rate for infants, while in the paper an article reported that the Secretary of Agriculture was investigating damage caused by the boll-weevil in the South. Wald reputedly declared: "If the Government can have a department to take such an interest in what is happening to the cotton crop, why can't it have a bureau to look after the nation's child crop?"

Like Hull-House in Chicago, the Henry Street Settlement on New York's Lower East Side was a compatible residence for Kelley. Both settlement founders—Addams and Wald—were committed to the well-being of children and, above all, opposed to child labor. A nurse by profession, Lillian Wald played a major role in organizing community-nursing in America, which became a model for "visiting nurses" worldwide. By 1916, she oversaw a Visiting Nurse Society in the city that tended to over a thousand patients a day, with private donations of more than a half million dollars a year. To Wald, there was "no finer manifestation [of nursing] than the care of the poor and disabled in their own homes" . . . in "five-story, walk-up, cold-water flats."

Health service provided by the visiting nurses covered "preventive, acute, and long-term care." It convinced the New York Board of Education to hire nurses for the city's schools, and Columbia University to appoint the first professor of nursing in the country. For her part, Kelley had advocated a National *Commission* for Children in her speeches since the turn of the century. And as Julia Lathrop pointed out years later: "In her book published in 1905, we find a plan for a United States Commission for Children whose scope and purpose were carried out in concise form in the 1912 Children's

Bureau Act." But its passage required six years of agitation, hearings, a White House Conference on Dependent Children, a federal study of women and children in industry, and the endorsement of Theodore Roosevelt—with strong resistance from states with industries relying on child labor.

Once Congress approved the Children's Bureau bill and President Taft signed it into law in April 1912, Addams informed Wald and Taft that "the Chicago group" favored Julia Lathrop to head the new office. Wald backed Lathrop, too, as "the best qualified person in the country for the job," and gained support for her in New York reform circles. Soon afterwards Taft made her "the first woman to lead a federal agency."

Her mandate as she saw it, was to "serve all children, to try to work out the standards of care and protection which shall give to every child [a] fair chance in the world." It had been argued that one voice—a single agency—could best meet the interests of the "whole child." Up until then children had been included in three distinct federal divisions: the departments of health, education, and the census.

The new act gave the Children's Bureau broad authority "to investigate and report upon all matters pertaining to the welfare of children and child life among all classes of our people . . . and especially [to] investigate the questions of infant mortality, the birth rate, orphanages, juvenile courts, desertion, dangerous occupations, accidents and diseases, employment . . . and legislation affecting children in the several States and Territories."

To begin with, an appropriation of $25,600 was allotted for a staff of fifteen to conduct "research and promotion." Upon consultation with key supporters—and staff selected according to the merit system—Lathrop decided first to concentrate on the problem of infant mortality, a subject of vital concern that seemed free of controversy. It readily became apparent that the death rate of infants was not known, nor was the birth rate upon which it was based, except for the records of a few states.

Yet babies continued to die, many of them because of the

"summer scourge" that had devastated mothers like Kelley's. A "baby-saving campaign" by the bureau was set in motion, with preliminary investigations in several cities and rural areas into the conditions existing for children born in a specific year—and following each child's history for twelve months.

The reports issued were jarring: the loss of babies in a year exceeded what was thought possible in America, as did that of "birth mothers." And it was demonstrated, to the degree one's income level increased, the infant and maternal death rate decreased. Kelley did not hesitate to publicize the findings, writing that:

> Earliest studies showed that six nations were more successful than we in keeping their babies alive to the first birthday; that our maternal death rate was the highest among civilized nations which kept records; and that a baby's chance of living was six times as good if its mother lived and could stay at home with it during its early weeks, as when she had to go back to the factory or do heavy work at home.

Lathrop made the decision to print a series of pamphlets on prenatal and infant care. While involving doctors, she had Mary Mills West, a widow with five children, prepare what turned out to be among the most popular publications put out by the government. The first, *Prenatal Care*, quickly ran out and could not keep up with the call for more. Almost a million and a half copies of the second, *Infant Care*, circulated in seven years; and the third, *Child Care and Milk,* was eagerly awaited and widely distributed. Meanwhile thousands of women across the country from all backgrounds were sending personal letters for help annually to the bureau, at the same time that magazines and newspapers vied for articles with advice on child welfare and other aspects of the bureau's work.

The General Federation of Women's Clubs volunteered to assist the bureau in its drive to carry out house-to-house birth registration and conduct accompanying surveys. A top priority for Lathrop, birth registration was fundamental to enforcing school attendance and child labor laws, as well as determining infant mortality and its causes. With a limited staff of its own, the Children's Bureau created a network of volunteer organizations to join in its campaign, notably Kelley's Consumers League, the National Child Labor Committee, Association of Collegiate Alumnae, Women's Christian Temperance Union, and the grass-roots Parent-Teachers Association—along with the Women's Club Federation.

Lathrop soon requested that the bureau's appropriation and staff be increased. When the House Appropriations Committee voted against it, she had only to notify supporters like Wald, Kelley, and Addams in order to activate the bureau's extensive network. Before long, their letters and telegrams poured-in to Congress, the press responded with editorials protesting the committee's vote, and indignant individuals reacted by expressing their own displeasure to officials. The extent of the outburst led the government to reconsider its refusal to increase funding—with the result that Lathrop's initial request was granted by an overwhelming majority.

Buoyed by its show of strength, the Children's Bureau took up the issue of child labor, documenting existing laws in each state and checking up on their enforcement. The 1900 census had recorded 1.75 million laboring-children "in mills, mines, fields, factories, stores, and on city streets," a large proportion of them under the age of fourteen, working up to twelve hours a day, sometimes seven days a week without time for school or play. A succession of bureau studies, starting in 1915, revealed a variety—and sometimes a lack—of labor rules and regulations in different parts of the country. Southern regions, especially those dominated by the textile industry, vehemently opposed government restrictions and openly violated what labor laws there were on the books.

The National Child Labor Committee—which included Kelley, Addams, and Wald on its board of directors—provided visual evidence of the perilous conditions for working children when it hired photographer Lewis Hine to depict scenes of child labor

(1908–1918). In one disturbing image, he shows "breaker boys" as young as ten hunched over in a mine shed, separating slate and stones from coal revolving on conveyer belts at their feet, malnourished and thinly clad.

In another picture—of a Gulf Coast cannery in the damp chill before dawn—"boys and girls, some seven and eight years old," stand shucking oysters beside adults, with "cloth finger stalls" to blunt the shells' sharp edges. And a day's work for the little cotton pickers he photographed in the South, Hine tells us, "follows the hot sun and not until sun-down do they leave for the night," trailing after their parents.

The "evils" of child labor became the focus also of muckrakers writing for *McClure's* magazine, *Cosmopolitan*, and *Collier's*; while Charles Dickens' ever-popular novel *Oliver Twist* about a workhouse-born-boy on the streets of industrial London (where the author himself had labored in a blacking factory at age twelve) struck a raw nerve in its readers. Child welfare advocates had long warned about the negative impact of young wage-earners denied "a right to childhood"—of children trapped in a cycle of ignorance, poverty, poor health, and all too often of breakdown or crime.

In response, the Keating-Owen Act was passed in 1916 and signed by President Wilson, ten years after being introduced in Congress. The first federal law to set restrictions on child labor, it did so by applying the interstate commerce clause of the *Constitution*. While supporters of the act had felt that the federal government might not be authorized to address child labor directly, they maintained that Congress did have the power to regulate it *indirectly* through interstate commerce.

In effect the act: "prohibited the interstate . . . shipment of materials produced in mines or quarries which employed children under sixteen years of age, products manufactured in facilities employing children under fourteen, or where children between the ages of fourteen and sixteen . . . worked more than eight hours a day, six days a week, or at night."

Approved in September 1916, the law was put in force a year

later—and lasted for 275 days before the Supreme Court found it unconstitutional. At its outset, Lathrop chose Grace Abbott—who took leave of the Immigrants Protective League in Chicago—to administer the law as director of the bureau's new Child Labor Division (thereby introducing a further dimension to the bureau's up-to-then purely research function).

The successful enforcement of a national minimum working age for the protection of children required "a good certificating system," which in turn relied upon birth records, skilled inspectors, and co-operation between the federal bureau and the states. In their short tenure, agents of the bureau helped inspect "689 factories in twenty-four states"—discovering a total of 294 factory violations.

Opponents of a child labor bill, who put states' and parents' rights before the power of the federal government to protect children, actively organized for the act's repeal from day-one of its passage. And prior to its enactment, a North Carolina judge pronounced it invalid in the Dagenhart case—on the grounds that it deprived the Dagenhart boys' father of his "right of property," namely, his two minor sons' labor in a cotton mill.

The following year by a 5–4 vote, the Supreme Court upheld the decision in *Hammer versus Dagenhart*, with the majority opinion stating that the law "not only transcends the authority delegated to Congress over commerce, but also applies a power to a purely local matter to which the federal authority does not extend."

In an "angry dissent," Justice Oliver Wendell Holmes declared that previous Supreme Court decisions—such as *Standard Oil versus the United States*—had established that Congress possessed broad powers to regulate interstate commerce. "The states may regulate their internal affairs and their domestic commerce as they like," he argued; "but when they seek to send their products across the state line they are no longer within their rights."

Six years later in a sequel to the case, the elder Dagenhart boy Reuben, now age twenty, exclaimed in an interview:

> Look at me! A hundred and five pounds, a grown man and no education. . . I think the years I've put in the cotton mills have stunted my growth. I had to stop school after the third grade . . . From 12 years old, I was working 12 hours a day—from 6 in the morning til 7 at night . . .

And he added:

> It would have been a good thing for all the kids in this state if that law they passed had been kept . . . But I know one thing. I ain't going to let them put my kid sister in the mill, like [my father's] thinking of doing. She's only 15 and she's crippled and I bet I stop that!

It should be recognized that children working in agriculture in rural areas—a majority of the count—remained unaffected by the Keating-Owen Act, as did young domestic workers (mainly girls) and those in the street trades. Moreover, given the seasonal nature of farm labor, children in remote regions generally attended school just three to six months during the year. Upon returning to the classroom after an absence, they found themselves far behind in their studies, often precipitating a final departure.

A second Child Labor Act, passed in 1919, used the federal government's taxing power as a strategy, imposing a tax of ten percent on the annual profits of goods produced in facilities employing children. Three years later it was invalidated as well, in a Supreme Court ruling stating that the federal taxing power could not serve the indirect purpose of regulating child labor. After two successive defeats of federal legislation, a constitutional amendment seemed the only way open to overcoming the court's blockage of unified child labor reform in America.

## *Sources*

Abbott, Grace. *Grace Abbott Reader*. Edited by John Sorensen, with Judith Sealander. Lincoln: University of Nebraska Press, 2008, 34.

Bremner, Robert H., ed., *Children and Youth in America: A Documentary History*, vol. II. Cambridge: Harvard University Press, 1971, 601–604, 716–717.

Davis, Allen. *Spearheads for Reform*. NY: Oxford University Press, 1967, 132–135.

Goldmark, Josephine. *Impatient Crusader: Florence Kelley's Life Story*. Urbana: University of Illinois Press, 1953, 78–108.

Hine, Lewis. *America & Lewis Hine: Photographs 1904–1940*. New York: Aperture Foundation, 1977.

Lindenmeyer, Kriste. *"A Right to Childhood."* Urbana: University of Illinois Press, 1997, 128–138.

Muncy, Robyn. *Creating a Female Dominion in American Reform*. NY: Oxford University Press, 1991, 55–65.

Wald, Lillian D. *Windows on Henry Street*. Boston: Little Brown & Company, 1934, chapter IV.

"Child labor and poverty are inevitably bound together and if you continue to use the labor of children as the treatment for the social disease of poverty, you will have both poverty and child labor to the end of time." — *Grace Abbott*

*A little spinner, regularly employed, Georgia, 1909.*

*Five-year-old newsie on Grand Avenue, St. Louis, 1910.*

*Nine-year-old tobacco picker, Connecticut, 1917.*

*"Dinner-toter" waiting for the gate to open, Georgia, 1913.*

*Little Lotte shucking oysters, Alabama, 1911.*

*Julia tending the baby at home, Alabama, 1911.*

*Jewel picking cotton, Oklahoma, 1916.*

*Twelve-year-old topping beets, 6am-6pm, with hour off at noon, Colorado, 1915.*

*Helper in glass factory, day shift one week, night shift the next, Georgia, 1911.*

*Bowery bootblack, New York, 1910.*

*Eight-year-old Daisy at capping machine, Delaware, 1910.*

*Small boy with a heavy load in Maryland packing company, 1909.*

"In the early days of my child labor activities I was an investigator with a camera attachment . . . but the emphasis became reversed until the camera stole the whole show." — *Lewis Hine, photographer*

*Addie, anemic spinner in Vermont cotton mill. She watches the whirling spools for breaks in the thread and mends them by tying the ends together, 1910.*

*Young marble worker running factory machine, Vermont, 1910.*

*Cutting sardines in cannery with large, sharp knives, Maine, 1911.*

*Drawing out a lathe tool at forge, Maryland, 1916.*

# Sweat-labor

*Embroidering in upper east side tenement, New York City, 1910.*

*Making artificial flowers, New York, 1924. Picture taken in connection with investigation.*

*Trapper boy in West Virginia mine, more than a mile inside. He opens and shuts a trap door to help ventilate the mine and clear it of gas, while allowing coal trucks through, 1908.*

*Boys in Pennsylvania breaker. Dust penetrates utmost recess of their lungs, 1911.*

*Midnight scene of thirteen-year-old in New Jersey glass works, 1911.*

# Pacifism and World War I

In August 1914, World War I erupted in Europe, set off by a Serb nationalist's assassination of the heir to the throne of Austria-Hungary. The incident in Sarajevo unleashed two armed European coalitions against each other, both of them bound by treaties:

> The *Allies*—Serbia, backed by Russia allied with France, England, and eventually Italy; and
> The *Central Powers*—Austria-Hungary, allied with Germany, and in time the Ottoman Empire and Bulgaria.

President Wilson proclaimed the United States' neutrality and offered his services as negotiator between the warring parties. Other neutral nations included Holland, Spain, Switzerland, and the Scandinavian countries. It was expected that the war would be short, that the troops would be "home by Christmas." But the fighting—much of it bloody trench warfare—lasted for four years with an estimated ten million military deaths and twice that number wounded. The harsh victory terms imposed by the Allies upon Germany had the effect of setting the stage for World War II, rather than making the Great War "the war-to-end-all-wars."

Addams and other advocates of peace found it "hard to believe that war had broken out between Germany and France, and later to receive the incredible news that England had also declared war." As she recalled it: "In our first horror against war we made an indict-ment comparing warfare to human sacrifice" and were astonished that "the comparison was received by our audiences as befitting the situation." In her view, warfare with thousands of young soldiers falling in battle amounted to "government sponsored murder."

In New York, Lillian Wald pronounced war "the doom of all that has taken years of peace to build up." Two decades of struggle for social justice were at stake, along with freedom of speech and the press. In her opposition to the use of force as a means for settling conflicts, she marched in a "parade of 1200 women down Fifth Avenue," and at the Henry Street Settlement, hosted the first of a series of meetings of social reformers committed to peace. Jane Addams had suggested convening it; and she would be instrumental, too, in organizing an Emergency Peace Federation in Chicago, a Woman's Peace Party in Washington, and a touring production of Euripides' *Trojan Women*, portraying not the "glory of war" but its "shame and blindness . . ."

Then in the spring of 1915 she was invited to attend an Inter-national Women's Conference in neutral Holland. Due to their disappointment over the wartime cancellation of that year's World Woman's Suffrage Congress in Berlin, a group of European women had decided to hold an International Congress of Women at The Hague, site of previous international peace initiatives. Altogether delegates from twelve countries participated in the April 28–May 1 conference, conceived as a protest against war. Before sailing, Jane Addams announced: "We do not think we can settle the war. . . . We do think it is fitting that women should meet and take counsel to see what may be done."

Suffragettes came from both belligerent and neutral nations, including Austria-Hungary (16 members), Belgium (5), Canada (2), Denmark (6), Germany (28), Great Britain (3, with some 180 denied travel permits), Italy (1), Holland (1,000), Norway (12), Sweden (16), and the United States (47). With France under attack, French women declined to take part. However two of the delegates from German-invaded-and-occupied Belgium provided a memorable moment when, upon entering the hall, they "shook hands with the German delegation before taking their places beside them on the platform."

Of the Americans, Jane Addams and Wellesley College professor Emily Balch assumed prominent roles. Alice Hamilton, Grace Abbott, and Sophonisba Breckenridge from the Hull-House community formed part of the United States' delegation as well. Like the women of warring nations, who encountered hostility at home and dangerous conditions in traveling to the congress, they faced criticism and the risk of a submarine attack in order to reach The Hague. To avoid the subject of blame for the war, it was agreed that talk of its causes and conduct would be off limits during the four days of sessions. But discussion of the terms of peace and the prevention of future wars "was carried on with much intelligence and fervor," according to Addams, who served as chair.

At the final gathering, resolutions were adopted, the most urgent one recommending that a Conference of Neutrals be called to negotiate an end to the war—preferably an official conference called by President Wilson, but if not, then an unofficial one with experts in international law. A core of "envoys"—among them Addams and Balch—were designated to visit fourteen capitals of neutral and belligerent nations to convey the results of the congress to them. Other key resolutions included the establishment of a society of nations and an international court of justice, disarmament and an end to secret treaties, voting rights for women, and a postwar meeting of The Hague delegates at the same time as the Peace Conference of world leaders (at Versailles).

After speaking with foreign ministers and heads of state, five of the envoys including the two American women issued a "Manifesto" in which they stated: "Our visits to the war capitals convinced us that the belligerent governments would not be opposed to a conference of neutral nations." Responses from each side to such a plan were quoted. For example:

My government would place no obstacle in the way of its institution.

Yours is the sanest proposal that has been brought to this office in the last six months.

It would be of the greatest importance to finish the fight by early negotiation rather than by further military efforts, which would result in more and more destruction and irreparable loss.

Neither side is today strong enough to dictate terms, and neither side is so weakened that it has to accept humiliating terms . . .Tentative propositions should first be presented by some outside power . . .

Since the war began, I've wondered many times why women have remained silent so long. As they are not expected to fight, they might easily make a protest against war which is denied to men.

And finally

What are the neutrals waiting for?

Addams expanded upon her own experiences in European capitals in a book *Women at The Hague*, to which Balch and Hamilton contributed. In her words: "We heard everywhere, in very similar phrases, that a nation at war cannot ask for negotiations nor even express a willingness for them, lest the enemy at once construe it as a symptom of weakness."

It seemed to her that the impetus for prolonging the war came mainly from the "animosity growing out of the conduct of the war . . . Germany indignant because England's blockade was an attempt to starve her women and children, England on fire over the German atrocities in Belgium" . . . and a young Frenchman "thinking of the poisonous gas and the horrible death of the men asphyxiated." In a papal audience, Pope Benedict XV had conveyed the Church view of the war as breeding "animosities which will tear down and rend to pieces the work of years."

During the Americans' visits to the wounded in hospitals, nurses reported that soldiers had informed them: "We can do nothing for ourselves but go back to the trenches so long as we are able. Cannot the women do something about this war?" And a youth on furlough declared to Addams, "We are told that we are fighting for civilization, but I tell you that war destroys civilization . . ." She learned, too, that "wounded lads, lying in helpless pain . . . call out constantly for their mothers . . ."

Before long she became aware of the existence of both a generational and a class gap—that is, "enthusiasm for the war was not as universal among the young men who were doing the fighting as it was among the elderly men established in the high places of church and state. It was the older men who had convinced themselves that this was a righteous war which must be fought to a finish."

But to her amazement, it was her comments at a Carnegie Hall speech regarding the soldiers' reaction to bayonet warfare that provoked a furor. As she related it, "In practically every country we'd visited, we had heard a certain type of young soldier say that it had been difficult for him to make the bayonet assault unless he had been stimulated; that the English soldiers had been given rum before such an attack, the Germans ether . . . and the French were said to use absinthe."

Charged with insulting the men by accusing them of lacking courage without stimulants, she replied that she had been misquoted by the press. For the audience at the meeting—she tried to point out—it had been clear that the drugs were distributed "not because the young men flinched at the risk of death, but because they had to be inflamed to do the brutal work of the bayonet, such as disemboweling, and were obliged to overcome all the inhibitions of civilization." Yet the die was cast. The press seized upon the bayonet story, making an issue of her patriotism.

When President Wilson did not act upon the European peace project that Addams put before him—despite thousands of telegrams from women's organizations seeking to stop the killing in Europe—the industrialist Henry Ford stepped in with a venture of his own: the Ford Peace Ship. Months later, in December 1915, his chartered ship set sail with great fanfare and a colorful crew on board—peace activists ranging from distinguished to eccentric, anti-war students, some celebrities, and a sizable contingent of the press.

Given the publicity surrounding the journey, the voyage soon overshadowed the conference, causing controversy over its "sensational" aspects. And once the ship arrived at its destination, Ford himself left—citing journalists' "misrepresentation" of his peace endeavor. Nonetheless the Conference of Neutrals took place in Stockholm as planned, culminating in an appeal for arbitration to both neutral and belligerent governments, and to their people. Addams followed the events from a Chicago hospital bed, ill with a recurrence of "tuberculosis of the kidney."

In her 1922 book *Peace and Bread in Time of War*, which recounted the war years, she reflected upon Wilson's transformation from "pacifist" to "warrior" in 1917: "It will always be difficult to explain the change in the President's intention (if indeed it was a change) occurring between his inaugural address on March 4th, and his recommendation for a declaration of war presented to Congress on April 2nd." Back in May 1915 in the wake of the German U-boat sinking of the British ocean liner *Lusitania,* with 128 American lives lost, he'd "refused to over-react."

The luxury ship, listed as "an auxiliary cruiser," was sailing under a neutral flag in a declared war zone, with a military cargo and orders to ram submarines. Wilson's Secretary of State, William Jennings Bryan, had warned against permitting passengers to travel on ships with contraband, in violation of international Cruiser Rules—and as leading the country to war.

The President's stirring "too proud to fight" speech at a citizen naturalization ceremony three days after the *Lusitania* was torpedoed, upheld and reaffirmed United States' neutrality in a strife-torn world:

The example of America must be the example not merely of peace because it will not fight, but of peace because peace is the healing and elevating influence of the world and strife is not. There is such a thing as a man being too proud to fight. There is such a thing as a nation being so right that it does not need to convince others by force that it is right.

Following intensive diplomacy, a curtailment of German submarine attacks resulted.

Throughout the 1916 presidential campaign the rallying cry had been: "He kept us out of war." Wilson's famous January 1917 address stating the conditions for a just and permanent peace had inspired optimism worldwide—as would his Fourteen Points speech a year later, which built upon attempts at a negotiated peace in wars of the past. His actions, though, increasingly focused on war preparation—on bases in the Caribbean and supply lines to Great Britain, leading to a renewal of German U-boat attacks.

In retrospect, Addams recalled a meeting with the President that pivotal March of 1917, during which: "He used one phrase . . . to the effect that, as head of a nation participating in the war, the President of the United States would have a seat at the Peace Table, but that if he remained the representative of a neutral country he could at best only 'call through a crack in the door.'"

As she interpreted it, his appeal to "war as an end to war" was being used as a flawed strategy for peace. "It was hard for some of us," she said, "to understand upon what experience this pathetic belief in the regenerating results of war could be founded." Grace Abbott, for one, spoke tellingly "of the futility of hoping against hope that justice might come out of . . . a struggle in which consideration of the wrongs of the oppressed had no part."

As an alternative to war, a delegation of peace representatives appealed to the President to look into what other American presidents had done "when the interests of American shipping had become involved in European wars—including George Washington during the French Revolution and John Adams in the Napoleonic War." In fact, international arbitration between Britain and the United States in 1794 over seizures of American ships trading with France, became known in Europe as "the American plan." If the present German attacks on American merchant ships were to be submitted to The Hague tribunal, it was suggested, it might mean "adjudication of the issues of the great war itself."

But by mid-summer, the first of two million American troops had disembarked in a France crippled by loss of life and livelihood. Russia, engulfed in revolution, was soon to exit the war. It was the fresh American troops, along with armaments from the world's now greatest industrial power, that determined the war's outcome. In November 1918, Germany surrendered, asking for an armistice on the basis of Wilson's "peace without victory"— which held that imposing a victor's terms upon the vanquished "would leave a sting, a resentment, a bitter memory upon which terms of peace would rest not permanently but only as upon quicksand."

The retaliatory treaty of the 1919 Versailles Peace Conference had that very effect, despite Wilson's presence at the peace table in defense of his program. Allied leaders bent on revenge undermined any hope of securing an enduring peace. Upon receiving a copy of the treaty, the Women's Peace Conference, meeting in Zurich, released a statement that proved to be prophetic:

> This International Congress of Women expresses its deep regret that the Terms of Peace proposed at Versailles should so seriously violate the principles upon which alone a just and lasting peace can be secured, and which the democracies of the world had come to accept.
>
> By guaranteeing the fruits of the secret treaties to the conquerors, the Terms of Peace tacitly sanction secret diplomacy, deny the principles of self-determination, recognize the right of the victors to the spoils of war, and create all over Europe discords and animosities, which can only lead to future wars.

By the demand for the disarmament of one set of belligerents only, the principle of justice is violated and the rule of force continued.

By the financial and economic proposals a hundred million people of this generation in the heart of Europe are condemned to poverty, disease and despair which must result in the spread of hatred and anarchy within each nation.

With a deep sense of responsibility this Congress strongly urges the Allied and Associated Governments to accept such amendments of the terms, as shall bring the peace into harmony with those principles first enumerated by President Wilson upon the faithful carrying out of which the honor of the Allied peoples depends.

As the Great War accelerated with the United States' entry in the spring of 1917, peacemakers on the home-front suffered a steady decline in their ranks. As long as the country remained neutral, Addams had been part of a peace movement based on collective action. But circumstances changed when war was declared against Germany. It became "every citizen's patriotic duty" to support the war effort; and she found herself at odds with the majority of Americans. Once considered the most admired woman in the country, her identification with the least popular cause of all—"peace in the time of war"—resulted in her reputation plummeting.

Newspapers routinely linked "the words traitor and pro-German with the word pacifist;" and the government waged an all-out campaign to justify the war, vilify those who spoke out against it, and prosecute anyone judged disloyal to the country under the wartime Espionage and Sedition Acts of 1917–1918. Addams then turned her attention to war relief on a federal level. As a volunteer for the Department of Food Administration headed by Herbert Hoover, she traveled widely "urging women to conserve food and help increase food production." Bread as a symbol for food had long been a concern of hers—going back to her father's flour mill in Cedarville, and her college essay on women as bread-givers.

———⊰ ⊱———

At the conclusion of the 1919 Women's Peace Congress, delegates renamed the organization the Women's International League for Peace and Freedom (WILPF). Addams was elected president—an office she continued to hold as long as her health permitted. At the invitation of the Quaker Friends Service, she then toured a devastated Germany, together with Alice Hamilton. It had been reported that starvation was ravaging Central Europe. As she told it:

> We had, of course, seen something of the widespread European starvation . . . Our first view of starved children was in the city of Lille in Northern France, where the children were being examined for tuberculosis . . . Their little shoulder blades stuck straight out, the vertebrae were all perfectly distinct, as were their ribs, and their bony arms hung limply at their sides.
>
> We were reminded of these children week after week as we visited Berlin, or Frankfurt am Main, or the cities of Saxony . . . An experience in Leipzig was typical when we visited a public playground in which several hundred children were having a noonday meal consisting of a pint of 'war soup,' of war meal stirred into a pint of hot water . . . The children would have nothing more to eat until supper, for which many of the mothers had saved the entire daily ration of bread . . . They hoped thus to avert the hardest thing they had to bear: hearing the children whimper and moan because they were too hungry to go to sleep.

It was the Quakers, the two women found, who were actively seeking to save as many Central Europeans as possible—those dealt a death sentence by the continuation of the English food blockade.

According to Hamilton:

> Everywhere they [Quakers] are received as the
> only people in the world whom everyone trusts, whom
> everyone knows to be disinterested, and all through
> the war they have worked on helping whomever they
> could reach and never admitting that any man was their
> enemy. . .

Upon her return to America, Addams gave a series of speeches to
raise money for the Quaker relief in Germany, although audiences
were generally unwilling to assist the defeated enemy. The newly
established League of Nations, for its part, was hindered in rendering
aid by a surge of nationalism among its members. In fact it appeared
to Addams "as if nationalism, through the terms of the Peace
Conference itself, had fallen back into an earlier psychology exhib-
iting a blind intolerance which [did] not properly belong to these
later centuries." The League, she felt, needed to find "a universal
motive" to overcome the divisiveness of postwar Europe and achieve
"genuine friendship and understanding"—as the suffrage women
had done in their wartime meetings for peace at The Hague and
Zurich.

Following the war, a Red Scare broke out in the United States
amidst the threat of "anarchist bombs and Bolshevik-provoked
conspiracies." Watch-lists of radicals were drawn up, a hunt for
"communists" conducted, and strikers branded as revolutionaries by
the press and public. Addams, Kelley, and Wald all incurred suspi-
cion and hostility for their anti-war activity, while labor—especially
striking immigrant labor—became subject to arrest and deportation,
most often on baseless charges.

Once President Wilson arrived home from Versailles in the summer
of 1919, he had before him the task of gaining Senate approval of the
peace treaty. In his view, the League's covenant was "the keystone of
the whole program." It called upon those who signed it: "to respect

and preserve against external aggression the territorial integrity and existing political independence of all members of the League."

The "victors' terms" of the settlement, he felt, could be corrected over time. But he insisted that the League—which encompassed an assembly, a council, and a World Court to maintain international peace—be an integral part of the treaty.

His Republican opponents, however, were determined to resist the League of Nations as an affront to American sovereignty. Congress, at first behind the President, changed—which caused him to take the matter directly to the people. The sheer exhaustion of embarking on a multi-city tour in the West led to his physical collapse, and to a stroke back in Washington. By March 1920, recovered enough to win support for the treaty by agreeing to submit its "vital matters" to congressional consent, he refused to do so; and his grand plan for peace went down to defeat. He did, though, receive the 1919 Nobel Peace Prize as the League's foremost architect.

In a little over a decade, in 1931, Addams too was notified that she'd been awarded the "Supreme Peace Prize" in Norway. She shared the honor with Columbia University President Nicholas Murray Butler—an incongruous match as he had "denounced those, like Addams, who opposed the war." At the time of her death—just four years later—the meaning she attached to her work for world peace would be expressed in the short but precisely-worded inscription she chose for her grave marker:

---

Jane Addams
of
Hull House
and
The Women's International League
for
Peace and Freedom

---

## Sources

Addams, Jane. *Peace and Bread in Time of War,* Urbana: University of Illinois Press, 2002. First published 1922. 36–42.

———. *Second Twenty Years at Hull-House.* New York: Macmillan, 1930, chapter 5.

Addams, Jane, Emily Balch, and Alice Hamilton, *Women at The Hague.* Urbana: University Press, 2003, xxvii–xxxiv, 27–46, 59–63, 78–81.

Berg, A. Scott. *Wilson.* NY: Putman's, 2013, 390-507, 511–678.

Commager, Henry Steele. *The Growth of the American Republic,* vol. 2. New York: Oxford University Press, 1980, xvi.

Costin, Lela. *Two Sisters for Social Justice.* Urbana: University of Illinois Press, 1983, 53–58.

Davis, A. F. *American Heroine.* NY: Oxford University Press, 1973, chapters XII, XIII, and 219, 251–261.

———. *Spearheads for Reform.* New York: Oxford University Press, 1967, 218–221.

Fischer, Marilyn. *On Addams.* Wadsworth Philosophers Series, 2004, 74–90.

Hamington, Maurice. *The Social Philosophy of Jane Addams.* Urbana: University of Illinois Press, 2009, 89–108 and chapter 5.

History of the International Court of Justice. UNESCO Archives: http://www.unesco.org/archives/new2010/index.html (accessed 2008).

Knight, Louise W. *Jane Addams: Spirit in Action.* NY: W.W. Norton, 2010, 187–188, 225–235, and chapter 6.

Sicherman, Barbara. *Alice Hamilton: A Life in Letters.* Cambridge: Harvard University Press, 1984, 226.

Wald, Lillian D. *Windows on Henry Street.* Boston: Little Brown & Company, 1934, chapter XII.

Wilson, Woodrow. "Address to Naturalized Citizens at Convention Hall." Philadelphia, May 1915. American Presidency Project, Document Archive: http://www.presidency.ucsb.edu/ (accessed 2008).

# CHAPTER 11

# The Twenties

## I. Grace Abbott, Second Head of the Children's Bureau

The twenties marked an end to the Progressive Movement and a "Return to Normalcy," to the status quo, and to laissez-faire (regulations-free) economics. It was a weary nation's response to the sacrifice and deprivation of war and a highly-regulated wartime economy. Republicans won a resounding victory in 1920. Their call for "Less government in business, [and] more business in government" fit the conservative postwar mood and stymied the forces of reform for a decade.

During the administrations of Harding, Coolidge, and Hoover, organized labor suffered setbacks in the steel industry, the coal mines, the railroads, and the textile factories. When strikes and conflicts broke out, the federal government and the courts supported management, usually by issuing injunctions and having the police back them up. A third-party alliance of farmers and labor, with progressive Senator La Follette from Wisconsin as its presidential candidate in 1924, failed to make headway, clearing the way for conventional policies and a record-breaking number of mergers.

As Secretary of the Treasury under all three Republican presidents, Andrew Mellon—one of the richest men in the United States—sealed the triumph of business through his fiscal program of cutting government expenditures and lowering taxes for wealthy industrialists and investors. Committed to the view that entrepreneurship would dry up without legislation to reward it, he held that the health of the nation depended upon a free market economy and the prosperity of the business class. Such a policy had the effect of increasing corporate profits, while wages lagged behind.

After 1924, "the Coolidge prosperity" spread its benefits in what became known as the Roaring Twenties, the Jazz Age, and the "big boom." But beneath the surface, its gains were not evenly distributed. Some forty percent of Americans had incomes of a subsistence level—reducing their purchasing power and resulting in a slowdown of industrial production. Wealth accumulation was then diverted into unbridled speculation.

Regions had to cope with downturns and changes of their own. New England, for instance, experienced a decline in its textile industry, which moved to the South for cheaper labor; and the Midwest suffered a severe farming depression. When the bubble of rising prosperity burst with the stock market crash of October 1929, Mellon's "economic miracle evaporated," and his "wizardry proved ineffective in averting a financial collapse."

Herbert Hoover—the President at the time the Great Depression hit—attributed the strength of the American system to "rugged individualism." A self-made man from a modest Quaker background, he'd risen to become an international engineer, a millionaire, the administrator of war relief, and Secretary of Commerce. In office, he pleased the business community by continuing the "policies of prosperity" of his Republican predecessors. His social philosophy stressed equality of opportunity through individual initiative, self-reliance, and voluntary co-operation rather than federal legislation. Well into the Depression, he viewed government intervention as a last resort.

With the enactment of the Nineteenth Amendment in 1920, the seventy-two-year-old campaign for woman's suffrage—dating from the first women's rights convention at Seneca Falls, New York in 1848—reached a successful conclusion. It was World War I and the contribution of women back home during wartime that provided the final stimulus to female suffrage in America. Given that the country was fighting for democracy in Europe, how could it exclude half its own citizens from the vote? Of the twelve nations represented at The Hague Women's Conference in 1915, nine from Europe, plus Canada, achieved enfranchisement by the time of the 1919 Peace Meeting in Zurich.

Addams first attended a National Suffrage Association Convention in 1906. In succeeding years, woman's suffrage became a leading cause for her, with countless speeches and articles addressing the arguments of its opponents—in particular, the traditional one that a woman's place was in the home and a man's in conducting the affairs of state. However in 1914 she resigned from the association's board due to its approval of "states-rights suffrage," which had racist undertones. Even the ratification of the Nineteenth Amendment did not make enfranchisement a reality for the majority of black women in the South, who were denied their legal right to vote by the poll tax, a literacy test, or other such restriction.

Still, why did it take so long for women to achieve suffrage? What were the reasons for the amendment's repeated defeat in state legislatures? In *Century of Struggle*, Eleanor Flexner's history of the woman's rights movement, the author poses the question: "Who Opposed Woman Suffrage?" and then proceeds to identify three major forces and the motivation behind each. The first, racism in the South, looked upon any extension of the Negro vote as a counterforce to white supremacy; while the second, "brewery" interests in the Midwest, felt threatened by women's support for prohibition. The third, big business in the East, anticipated added pressure for government regulation of industry.

—³ ⁸—

As it turned out, ratification of the Nineteenth Amendment did not result in female voters joining together to pass expected reforms. Nor were politicians removed from office for ignoring the issues of child health and child labor. Grace Abbott—who followed Lathrop as head of the Children's Bureau in 1921—had taken it for granted that "all reasonable people" would respond to the bureau's programs for infant and maternity health care and child labor legislation. When that proved not to be the case, this determined daughter of Nebraska pioneers—who'd experienced severe drought, debt, and the prolonged depression of the 1890s—accepted then, as she would in the future, "temporary defeat in the confident belief of ultimate victory, even when the odds on the other side are very great."

Her sister Edith—the first woman dean of a university graduate school—wrote movingly of their childhood on the prairie in *A Sister's Memories*:

> Grace and I often talked over the vivid memories which we shared of the pioneer days in our part of the Great Plains . . . And we used to say that if we lived in Chicago a hundred years, we would never forget the call of the meadow larks along the roadside; the rustling of the wind in the corn; the slow flight of the sand-hill cranes over the prairie creek near our home; and the old Overland Trail, a mile from the main street of our town...

Both parents grew up in DeKalb County in northern Illinois. Othman Abbott fought in the Civil War, studied law, and traveled west in a covered wagon, ending up in frontier Grand Island (between two channels of the Platte River) in the new state of Nebraska. The first lawyer in those parts, he "drew up the charter for the city," served in the state senate, and became Nebraska's first lieutenant governor. His wife "Lizzie" Gardner had Quaker roots; her family had kept a station on the Underground Railroad for run-away slaves. A graduate of Rockford Seminary, she taught school before her marriage, rose to be principal, and was a committed suffragist. Looking back, her girls felt they had been "born believing in women's rights."

To Grace, their small western town was—in her words—"the most honestly democratic place in the world. There were no people who were rich, and the poor we all knew as individuals . . . people who had had one misfortune or another . . . whom we should try to help." Like their mother—and their Quaker grandmother who lived with them—the Abbott daughters were concerned about injustice, conscious of the "sorrowful trail of dispossession" of the plains Indians and proud of the ardent anti-slavery tradition on both sides of their family. In the controversy over an equal rights' amendment in the 1920s, they supported low-wage-earning women who had need of protective legislation—workers that business-and-professional women neglected in their struggle for equality.

Their father shared the "excitement and satisfaction" of his law practice with Grace and Edith, inviting them to the courthouse to follow cases of special interest. The experience left Grace aspiring to become a lawyer herself; and in later life, of remembering the county court as a "substitute for the movies." In the Abbott household, an atmosphere of "stimulating discussion and lively debate" reigned. The "best books" were read, the girls were encouraged to speak their minds, and acting independently was highly valued. Because of economic hardship, advanced education had to be delayed while the two sisters taught school for extended periods and pursued their college degrees over time.

It was in 1907 at age twenty-nine that Grace arrived for graduate study in political science at the University of Chicago, where she received her master's degree. Edith had preceded her in 1902 for a doctorate in economics. By 1908, the two young women were living at Hull-House, where they remained for ten productive years as a part of the settlement's "inner circle." Both were naturally "at home" in the Progressive Movement—Grace as a defender of women, children, and immigrants; and Edith as a researcher and scholar. According to Edith, "I could assemble the facts and write a report, but Grace had the gift of applying the proper legislative remedy."

As Julia Lathrop's chosen successor to the Children's Bureau in 1920, Grace had the responsibility of implementing the Sheppard-Towner Maternity and Infancy Act—the first system of federal aid for social welfare in the country. Built upon Lathrop's earlier infant mortality studies, the act authorized "an annual appropriation of a million and a quarter dollars over a five-year period" as federal matching funds for the states to set up "well-baby and parent education programs," especially in outlying rural areas. Thus, as Edith noted, public health nurses began to appear in places "where they'd never been heard of before."

> They visited the homes of infants and preschool children and expectant mothers, established health centers, organized conferences, promoted campaigns for breast feeding and for birth registration, assisted with immunization work, and organized talks, leaflets, motion pictures, and lantern slides. Grace even developed plans to use the newly developed medium of radio broadcasting [her sister recounted].

Both Lathrop and Grace—who worked on drafting the bill—were clear that they didn't want a charity program of "poor relief," but a community service to give children of all classes a good start in life. Nearly thirty percent of draftees for World War I had been found unfit for military service; and wartime efforts had been undertaken to develop minimum standards for child health.

Sheppard-Towner relied heavily on the co-operation of the states. As Grace explained it:

> It intends . . . that [maternity and infant] plans shall originate in the States, and they ought, of course, to be carefully adapted to meet local needs. The plans that have been submitted show much diversity, and yet there is in them all the same fundamental conception of the problem . . . First, to secure an appreciation among women of what constitutes good prenatal and obstetrical care, and Second, how to make available adequate community resources . . .

One condition was that funds had to go to public agencies as "public services for children and women." It was up to Abbott to collaborate successfully with state and local officials—as she had done in 1917–1918 administering child labor legislation for the bureau. By the end of 1923, just seven of the forty-eight states had failed to accept the bill's terms. When Sheppard-Towner ended in 1929, only three holdout states remained; and birth registration approached ninety-five percent.

The act illustrated both the dangers women faced in pregnancy and childbirth, and the influence an effective lobby of women's organizations could command. Those loyal to the bureau had striven all-out for the bill's passage, with stiff resistance from anti-suffrage and anti-government forces, and from the American Medical Association (AMA), protective of its own interests. Precedents for a grant-in-aid program included previous legislation providing federal matching funds to the states for agricultural assistance, highway construction, and vocational education.

Women overwhelmingly staffed the Children's Bureau office and served as physicians and nurses. On the state level, some "seventy-five percent of Sheppard-Towner administrators were female, [as were] the more than eight hundred state board of health nurses . . . half the act's doctors and the majority of other paid and voluntary positions." No woman, though, directed a state board, and as a rule men occupied positions of policy in Washington departments—except in the Children's Bureau.

Federal action in administering Sheppard-Towner had been confined to advocacy and education. It was the role of the states and local communities to deliver affordable health care to mothers and babies. During the act's seven years of existence, awareness of infant and maternal mortality grew steadily, with the states operating some three thousand well baby and prenatal health centers, and co-sponsoring an estimated 120,000 child health conferences for a million-and-a half children.

Defenders of Sheppard-Towner failed to win its renewal in 1927 amidst Coolidge's fiscally conservative government, which agreed to finance its extension for two years only, from 1927 to 1929. At a 1930 White House conference on health and hygiene called by President Hoover, the bureau's network of women advocates fought together against a report recommending transfer of the

Children's Bureau health division to the Public Health Service—a move backed by the AMA. Conflict erupted at the meeting when Abbott's minority report opposing the transfer was read, with an overflowing female audience registering their disapproval of change and causing the recommendation to be withdrawn.

For women devoted to child welfare, the exclusive American Medical Association proved a formidable foe. As social historian Robyn Muncy specified: "It was male rather than female; profit-seeking instead of service-oriented; [and] it aimed to hoard rather than popularize its expert knowledge." Moreover as a monopoly, the AMA "competed against non-medical professionals, while the women depended on co-operation" among professions. Significantly, "female doctors refused to focus their attention exclusively on the medical aspects of disease . . . also exploring the 'effects of poverty, sanitation, housing conditions, industrial processes, and nutrition upon health.'" Birth control remained an "off-limits" subject, and daycare a controversial one at a time when the middle-class value of a working father and a stay-at-home mother prevailed.

Meanwhile a strenuous and resourceful effort led by Abbott resulted in a child labor amendment to the *Constitution* being passed in 1924 and sent to the states with high hopes for its ratification. As worded, it gave Congress the power "to limit, regulate, and prohibit the labor of all persons under the age of eighteen." However the amendment failed over time to secure the vote of the three-fourths of states required for its enactment. Manufacturers that employed children, "patriots" who denounced regulation as socialistic, and the Catholic Church, which feared the "nationalization of education," all voiced strong opposition.

Historically, the fight against child labor has stood in the forefront of industrial reform. To quote Abbott:

> The child labor movement has in every country
> supplied the shock troops in the struggle for decent

working conditions. The victories secured in the early child labor laws opened the way for general regulation of factory conditions and demonstrated the necessity for a factory-inspection system. Child labor laws were also a pioneering effort on the part of the state to insure to children a national minimum standard . . .

And in assessing the progress of women's rights on the tenth anniversary of the ratification of the Suffrage Amendment, she reflected on the slow advance made by women in attaining government positions—then ended on a positive note:

> Some women and some men wonder why change in the position of woman has been desired. Repeatedly they ask, "Why should anyone choose the 'strenuous life'? Why seek a part in the struggle to end the injustice and ugliness of our modern life?" They are the lotus-eaters who prefer to live in a gray twilight in which there is neither victory nor defeat. It is impossible for them to understand that to have had a part in the struggle— to have done what one could—is in itself the reward of effort and the comfort in defeat.

## Sources

Abbott, Edith. "A Sister's Memories," *Social Service Review.* University of Chicago, 1939, 351–407.

Abbott, Grace. *From Relief to Social Security.* NY: Russell and Russell, 1966. First published in 1941. 4–5.

———. *Grace Abbott Reader.* Edited by John Sorenson, with Judith Sealander. Lincoln: University of Nebraska Press, 2008, xxv–xxvi, 36, 38, 103, 112.

Commager, Henry Steele. *Growth of the American Republic*, vol. 2. New York: Oxford University Press, 1980. chapter XVII.

Costin, Lela B. *Two Sisters for Social Justice.* Urbana: University of Illinois Press, 1983, 5, 9–10, 39, chapters 4–7.

Flexner, Eleanor and Ellen Fitzpatrick. *Century of Struggle.*
    Cambridge: Harvard University Press, 1996. First published
    1959. chapter 22.

Goldmark, Josephine. *Impatient Crusader: Florence Kelley's Life
    Story.* Urbana: University of Illinois Press, 1953, 108–120.

Greenleaf, William. *U.S.A. The History of a Nation*, vol. 2. Chicago:
    Rand McNally, 1969, chapters 12 and 19.

Knight, Louise. *Jane Addams: Spirit in Action* (NY: W. W. Norton).
    2010, 149–151, 237.

Lindenmeyer, Kriste. *"A Right to Childhood": The U.S. Children's
    Bureau and Child Welfare, 1912–46.* Urbana: University of
    Illinois Press, 1997, 105–107.

Muncy, Robyn. *Creating a Female Dominion in American Reform.*
    NY: Oxford University Press, 1991, 136–148.

Schlesinger, Jr, Arthur. *Crisis of the Old Order: 1919–1933.* Boston:
    Houghton Mifflin, 1957, 49–89.

## II. Edith Abbott, Dean of the University of Chicago's School of Social Service Administration

The "Abbott sisters of Nebraska," as they were sometimes referred to by friends and associates, had distinctive personalities even as children, despite many characteristics in common. As their biographer Lela Costin described it:

> Edith was highly sensitive and somewhat fearful; she was anxious for parental approval, tended to cling to home, and loved learning and scholarship. Books were a treasure to her. Grace in turn was more adventuresome and self-confident, more able to question and oppose her parents. Learning to her was highly important . . . to find an answer on which to act.

Artistic and literary, Edith wrote perceptively of nature on the prairie—of the "endless frozen, pathless winters of those early years and the wonderful time when, at long last, 'spring came on forever.'" She told too of the "long summer twilights when we climbed high up on the cottonwood trees to watch the prairie fires creeping along the distant horizon." But the old frontier disappeared with time, "vanished"—as she expressed it—"like the beautiful herd of antelope that my father used to see from the door of his first law office—antelope grazing on the buffalo grass of the plains."

Upon graduating from the Brownell Boarding School in Omaha with a Gold Scholarship Medal at age sixteen, Edith traveled with Grace to visit the 1893 World's Fair in Chicago. It was a carefully-planned and saved-for gift from their mother; and with drought and depression gripping Nebraska, amounted to "almost our last reasonably carefree outing for a long period of years," Edith recalled. She singled out the sight of the "new university," visible from the fair, as a highlight of the trip. A decade of economic struggle—teaching interspersed with correspondence and summer courses, and a final year spent at the University of Nebraska—would pass before she returned for a graduate degree at the, by-then, prominent Chicago university.

Othman Abbott suffered "crippling debt" during the nineties, but resisted bankruptcy and slowly paid off what he owed from bank and business failures. It took a toll on his family, yet the plight of the farmers was far worse. The parched earth meant a loss of crops, starving livestock, and near famine for the rural population, demanding all the courage and fortitude of their pioneering past to survive. To Edith, her father represented the "best of the old rugged individualists." The Abbotts' western heritage stood out as a matter of pride for her—a heritage that enabled the people of the plains to meet challenges, persist, and in the end rise above great adversity.

At the co-educational University of Chicago, Edith and then Grace chose non-traditional courses for women—in fields like economics, political science, and law. Among the offerings that attracted Edith was one on the "legal and economic position of women," taught by Sophonisba Breckinridge, a future friend and colleague. From a distinguished Kentucky family, her great-grandfather had been Thomas Jefferson's attorney general; and her own father served in Congress as a liberal Southern Democrat. Supportive of education for women, he approved of the choice she made to attend Wellesley College in New England. After graduating, she determined to become an attorney—and succeeded in being the first woman in Kentucky admitted to the bar.

But disheartened by the lack of clients seeking a female lawyer, she responded to an opportunity to pursue advanced studies in politics and law at the University of Chicago with the legal scholar Ernst Freund. Trained in German historicism—which viewed law in its social and historical context—he introduced her to a wider, more activist approach to the field, one that addressed the conditions of industrial society. Freund's dynamic conception of law evolving through time provided a basis for the enactment of social legislation "to promote the public welfare." His justification of government intervention in the interests of "a greater good" set the foundation for Breckinridge's lifetime involvement with reform and the establishment of a humane welfare system.

Yet the prospects for women with doctorate degrees in social science of securing university positions were not promising. At Chicago, it was in a less academically challenging appointment as instructor in the Department of Household Administration that Breckinridge found the employment denied her in the male strongholds of political science and economics. She had accepted the "female oriented" job offered her in order to remain at the university, where she could carry on her investigations, teach, and "develop new resources in the city that made life an ongoing adventure." Increasingly dedicated to civic reform, she joined the Chicago division of the Women's Trade Union League, and utilized her legal background to try to gain protective legislation for working-class women.

It was to a considerable extent Breckinridge's contacts that led to Edith Abbott's postgraduate work in Boston for the Women's Trade Union League and the American Economic Association—which was followed by research at the Carnegie Institute in Washington on the history of women workers. Her statistical account of the long record of female participation (and exploitation) in the labor force—from colonial times to the twentieth century—culminated five years later in a ground-breaking book *Women in Industry*, with a preface by Breckinridge and a dedication to her.

A year in England at the London School of Economics with Carnegie funds (1906–1907) transported Edith into a new world of socialism, debate over the Poor Law, and radical woman's suffrage. Sidney and Beatrice Webb were major figures at the school; and as Fabian socialists, they concentrated upon "research and education." Like their political namesake Fabius, who as a third-century B.C. Roman general fought Hannibal's superior Carthaginian army by wearing it down with "delay and harassment," rather than military force, they hoped to bring about a socialist state through gradual expansion, not direct confrontation. Symbol of the Fabian Society was the tortoise.

During Edith's stay in London, the Webbs voiced their strong objection to the Poor Law relief system under review by a Royal Commission, of which Beatrice was a prominent member. It was her 1909 Minority Report recommending universal public services, as well as an end to the repressive Poor Law, which presented one of the first accounts of a modern welfare state. She set forth "a national minimum of civilized life . . . open to all alike, of both sexes and all classes," with "sufficient nourishment and training when young, a living wage when able-bodied, treatment when sick, and a modest but secure livelihood when disabled or aged." Such progressive proposals as employment exchanges, improved education, universal health care, and a minimum wage, were embodied in the plan.

In opposition, the Majority Report took a limited view of Poor Law reform, one that advocated creating new county authorities, along with separate institutions for poorhouse inmates falling under different categories (children, the old, the unemployed, and the mentally-ill). After winning the general elections of 1906 and 1910, the new Liberal Party government ignored poor relief proposals and with the support of Labor was able to pass welfare measures of its own, including introductory forms of health and unemployment insurance. Influenced by the success of Bismarck's social program in Germany, party leaders felt rebellion would break out in England if labor conditions failed to improve.

For the Webbs, the source of poverty was structural in the economic system, not the fault of individuals in need of personal improvement. A decade earlier Booth's investigation of the poor in London's East End had found "illness and old age" to be responsible for more poverty than "idleness and moral weakness." In future years, Edith's Chicago students would learn of the controversy created during the English Poor Law review, through lectures and readings putting America's fledgling public relief system in perspective.

England's militant suffrage movement was addressed by Abbott in an article expressing renewed hope for the feminist cause—inspired by the active participation in London suffrage demonstrations of women from the textile factories. And an encouraging message arrived from America of the opening of an appointment for her in the Economics Department at Wellesley College. But the picturesque women's school in Massachusetts—whose faculty Abbott joined in the fall—proved not entirely to her liking. After the "bracing atmosphere" that she'd experienced in London and Chicago, she preferred a big city research university to a liberal arts school in a "sleepy college town." Moreover at Chicago, the women students seemed more serious than the Wellesley girls she encountered "racing down the main corridors of College Hall" and "coming to lectures in gymnasium shirts and shorts . . ."

A return to Chicago was realized the next year when—again at the instigation of Sophonisba Breckinridge—she joined the Chicago School of Civics and Philanthropy in its new research department, made possible by a grant from the Sage Foundation. It was a bold step to leave a secure position at a well-known eastern college, for a social work training school in the Midwest that was not affiliated with any academic institution. However the move allowed her to investigate problems integral to industrial life—to undertake scientific studies of housing, juvenile delinquency, and vocational training, for example; and to live at Hull-House with her sister Grace.

The country's foremost settlement then included some "twenty-five women and twelve men residents, along with several married couples, all of varying professions and interests—music teachers, artists, club leaders, social workers, lawyers, journalists, physicians, and a few successful businessmen who wanted to work with a social reform group." According to Edith:

> Our political views differed widely, and our arguments not infrequently began at the breakfast table, and during the day the various participants in the current controversy seemed to have sharpened their weapons and prepared for the new arguments that were sure to be heard at the dinner table.

Discussion often continued late in the evening when activities for the neighbors ended.

—⸱ ⸱—

In the fall of 1908, Breckinridge succeeded Julia Lathrop as director of the new Department of Social Investigation in the Chicago School of Civics and Philanthropy, with Abbott appointed assistant director. Due to the lack of formal education available for social workers at the time, the program the two women developed drew significantly upon their own graduate work in social science.

An early housing survey to examine living conditions in the city came at the request of Chicago's sanitary inspector. Both Abbott and Breckinridge had direct experience of immigrant tenements and urban blight through their association with Hull-House. Moreover Breckinridge played a leading role in establishing the Immigrants' Protective League, and was largely responsible for Grace Abbott being chosen to administer it.

During the housing investigation, students trained in methods of social inquiry pursued research under their directors' supervision. A door-to-door canvas was undertaken to inspect dwellings and interview tenants of designated districts, with a detailed account kept of each visit. Often cramped furnished-rooms in tenements would be windowless, the plumbing non-existent, and privacy unknown. Health standards and building codes generally remained unenforced. Nowhere was disease more rampant and the situation more "demoralizing" than in the area behind the Stock Yards' slaughterhouses, where Slavic immigrants experienced some of the worst lodging in Chicago.

But it was the blacks in the city that suffered the most, segregated and discriminated against at every turn. Always sensitive to the race problem, Breckinridge made an issue of including black "ghettos" in the survey. She felt confident that once the "great majority of whites" learned the extent of the injustice inflicted upon the Negro, they would want to alleviate it. Research resulting in clear-cut statistical data seemed—to her—a way of countering racism. In addition, she took personal action by joining the Chicago NAACP and seeking support for the Wendell Phillips House, a settlement for blacks.

A collaborative study by Breckinridge and Abbott—*The Delinquent Child and the Home* (1912)—dealt with Chicago's juvenile court system. Case histories of more than a decade were reviewed, probation officers consulted, and meetings arranged with a sampling of families of children appearing in court in a particular year. Findings stressed the environmental factors of delinquency, above all, poverty as a root cause. A related project, *Truancy and Non-Attendance in the Chicago Public Schools* (1917), looked into the effectiveness of compulsory education laws and child labor legislation. Here too, it was impoverished children in distressed households that were at risk—called on to fill in for an ailing parent, put to work to add to a family's meager earnings, or left to drift on their own, to their detriment. City schools lacked thousands of placements in immigrant districts, while child labor laws in the state were laxly enforced and routinely evaded.

To Edith, her year's experience in London offered an example of social reform that was not constrained by the "constitutional limitations" existing in her own country. She kept track of the progress of welfare measures in England where parliament had the last word, most notably the regulation of child labor and of wages—measures which federal courts regularly invalidated in the United States. A family's loss of income from abolishing child labor could be remedied, Abbott and other reformers maintained, by raising the wages of adult workers. Back in the nineties, Addams had sought funds to keep struggling widows' children in school from whatever sources she could, public or private.

By 1915 the School of Civics and Philanthropy was showing signs of acute financial strain, as the Sage Foundation grant approached its expiration. To Abbott and Breckenridge, affiliation of the school with a major university appeared to be the best all-around solution. Such a move became a reality in 1920, when the University of Chicago's trustees authorized a Graduate School of Social Service Administration. For the two women academics, no better outcome could have been envisioned.

In 1924 Edith was made dean of the new graduate school, the first in social work to be part of an important research university. During the early years of the field, preparation had consisted of an apprenticeship to a charity or public welfare institution. Over time, a few training schools in cities like Chicago, New York, and Boston added coursework. After World War I, caseworkers began to concentrate upon psychiatry as a means of gaining insight into their clients' problems, a development resisted by Abbott. She sought rather to enact "a solid and scientific curriculum in social welfare," along with casework and investigative research, although she did include a psychiatric social worker on her staff.

With Grace serving as chief of the Children's Bureau from 1921 to 1934, the sisters had an opportunity to work together from their respective strengths. Thus Edith conducted studies for the bureau, to assist Grace in administering crucial public programs. Such a relationship had existed during their Hull-House years as well, with Grace's leadership of the Immigrants Protective League and Edith's research on immigration with the School of Civics and Philanthropy. Given their mutual trust and understanding—along with the values and goals they shared—it was only after consulting with one another that either arrived at an important policy decision or embarked on a new initiative.

In her biography, Costin distinguished the two women during their mature years:

> Each worked tremendously hard, Edith more intensely without the relief that might have spared her serious headaches and other forms of stress. Each had a quick wit, but Edith's often had a biting edge, while Grace's was of the kind that in any discussion cleared the air, cut through any person's self-assumed importance, and brought about a more relaxed perspective on the

question at hand—even as she bore in with a reminder of the data and a proposed line of action.

A professional journal, the *Social Service Review*, was begun in 1927, with scholarly research on a range of social problems—and a series of public documents, case studies, and graduate theses published as background sources. When at age thirty, Robert Hutchins arrived in Chicago as the new president of the university in 1929, Edith discovered that they had much in common concerning their views on education. Both held that a university should turn out educated persons, not apprentices prepared for a job. Neither approved of the trend toward "careerism that stressed the training of technicians in the professions."

According to Hutchins:

> Very early, Miss Abbott convinced me that the social work profession had an intellectual content that had to be mastered in itself and that her intent was to turn out individuals who understood both the social science base and the special content of social work.

He further noted that she could hold her own in deans' meetings, and often dominated discussions. As he put it, her influence was attributable to "the clarity and force of her mind" and not to any prestige of social work, which would not be acknowledged by that "august assembly of males." He characterized her as being "extremely direct, never bothering to try to indulge in circumlocution for the purpose of making what she said more agreeable. She simply said [what she had to say] in the simplest possible language, and she was always enormously effective."

As a teacher in the classroom, she was likewise impressive, with high standards and an intensity that made students feel "involved in the causes in which she was engaged and ready to do battle by her side." One of them spoke of her "tremendous dedication to right what was wrong," and another of how demanding she was and of how they responded "because she expected it of us." To many, it was a familiar sight to see her walking on campus in conversation with her close associate Sophonisba Breckinridge (they were often referred to as "A and B").

As the two were pictured:

> Their preoccupation and leisurely pace gave them a pathway to themselves. Students walked around them on the grass. These diminutive Victorian ladies seemed larger because of their [long dark dresses] …Their faces were almost obscured by their hats.

In the preface to her 1931 book *Social Welfare and Professional Education*, Edith expressed her "deep obligation . . . to my sister, Grace Abbott . . . and to my long-time colleague and friend, Professor Sophonisba Preston Breckinridge . . ." She credited the "joint thinking of the three of us" as responsible for a "common interest we have had since the days when we all lived at Hull-House and worked together at the University and on the West Side of Chicago."

> For it was through this joint service [she continued] that we first came to see the great importance of bringing the University to the service of the problems of social welfare, to the end that, on the one hand, humanitarian work may become more scientific, and, on the other, that the work of the social scientist may be quickened and strengthened by being brought to the service of humanity.

At that period, it should be inserted, a professional career and marriage were rarely combined by college-educated women—who turned out to be of the generation "least likely to wed in American history." College graduates predominated among those females remaining single. Both Abbotts chose to forego marriage, although Edith was a beautiful young woman and Grace enjoyed mixed outings in her Nebraska years. Discovering themselves excluded from male-oriented careers, they devoted themselves wholeheartedly to developing the new fields of social work and public welfare—professions that seemed fitting as well as accessible.

Although her schedule was always full, in 1929 Edith oversaw President Hoover's Wickersham Commission investigation "of crime and the foreign-born." Upon making an intensive study with a staff of her choosing, she determined that in proportion to their numbers, the foreign-born were responsible for fewer crimes than those who were natives. The report further revealed an anti-immigrant mood in the country that scapegoated "foreigners" and would result in deporting some two million Mexicans during the Depression.

According to Abbott:

> For more than a century there has been . . . a clamorous group who have tended to emphasize only the difficulties connected with immigration and to lose sight of all its beneficial effects. Unfortunately these attacks . . . have frequently laid stress on the popularly supposed relation between immigration and crime. Statistics have never justified their assumptions . . .

## Sources

Abbott, Edith. "The Hull-House of Jane Addams." *Social Service Review*, Chicago, Sept. 1952.

———. *Social Welfare and Professional Education*. Chicago: University of Chicago Press, 1931, viii–ix.

———. *Women in Industry*. NY: Appleton & Company, 1910, chapters XII–XIII.

Abbott, E. and Breckinridge, S. P. *Truancy and Non-Attendance in the Chicago Schools*. NY: Arno Press & the *New York Times*, 1970. First published in 1917. 346–353.

Costin, Lela. *Two Sisters for Social Justice: A Biography of Grace and Edith Abbott*. Urbana: University of Illinois Press, 1983, 6, 12–14, 18–19, 24, 58–67, 98–102, and chapters 2, 8.

Fitzpatrick, Ellen. *Endless Crusade: Women Social Scientists and Progressive Reform*. NY: Oxford University Press, 1990, 20–25, 66–69, 87–91, 209–215, and chapter 7.

Mennel, Robert. *Thornes and Thistles: Juvenile Delinquency in the United States, 1825–1940.* Hanover, NH: University Press of New England, 1973, chapter 5.

# The New Deal

Despite the deepening of the Depression, President Hoover delayed distributing reconstruction funds provided by Congress as "relief loans to the states," until local and private assistance had been depleted. Both Abbott sisters documented the impact of pervasive unemployment and poverty upon "children, families, 'transient boys,' and the homeless." Edith equated placing the responsibility for disaster-relief upon charity, with a return to the English Poor Law of the sixteenth century; while Grace's survey of malnutrition and deprivation in mining families, exposed the failure of philanthropy to cope with the devastation.

With Roosevelt's New Deal administration, both women applauded the choice of Frances Perkins as Secretary of Labor—the first female in American history to serve in a presidential cabinet. As a social worker and secretary of Florence Kelley's Consumers League in New York City, Perkins's "personal call to action" had occurred in 1911 when she witnessed the tragic Triangle Shirtwaist Factory fire. One-hundred-and-forty-six girls, mainly from Jewish and Italian immigrant families, died "behind locked doors, or leaping, screaming, to the streets [eight-to-ten stories] below."

Appointed a member of the commission to conduct an inquiry into the fire, Perkins provided information on worker safety and health, and showed the commissioners some unforgettable scenes of "callous child labor" and "thousands of women, pale and exhausted, coming off a ten-hour night shift on ropewalks."

During Roosevelt's years as New York governor, Perkins had

served as the state's Industrial Commissioner; and when it became known that she was being considered for the cabinet position of Secretary of Labor, a deluge of supportive telegrams and letters arrived at the newly-elected President's office—above all from social workers and women's organizations. A previous nationwide campaign for Grace Abbott to become labor secretary under President Hoover, while unsuccessful, paved the way for Perkins's selection not long afterwards.

Having learned to navigate her way effectively in Washington, Grace took it upon herself to introduce the new cabinet member to congressional representatives, the press, and the Labor Department itself—of which the Children's Bureau was a part. Perkins later said that she had found her to be "an invariable authority on the whole department," one who had given "long and practical thought to its problems." Her advice was so sound, Perkins stated, "that I recognized her more often than any one else."

From 1933 to 1939, Abbott acted as an advisor to the Secretary of Labor. She helped prepare the Social Security Act of 1935 as well—testifying in congressional hearings and drafting programs on "aid to dependent children, services for the disabled child, and maternal and infant health." With respect to the Fair Labor Standards Act three years later, Perkins reported in her book *The Roosevelt I Knew*:

> One last minute change was the insertion of a clause prohibiting the labor of youngsters under sixteen in industries engaged in interstate commerce or affecting interstate commerce, and providing for not more than eight hours of work a day for children over sixteen. As Grace Abbott, Chief of the Children's Bureau, so eloquently pleaded, "You are hoping that you have found a way around the Supreme Court [in its overturning of New Deal legislation]. If you have, why not give the children the benefit by attaching a child labor clause to this bill?"

But how did the phenomenon of child labor become entrenched in a democracy? And what took its prohibition so long to come? In the *Grace Abbott Reader,* a chapter entitled "Why Did Child Labor Ever Develop in America?" attempts to answer such questions. Throughout the colonial period, as Abbott explains it, there had been a belief "in the virtue of industry and the sin of idleness, even in children." However she specifies that it was Treasury Secretary Alexander Hamilton who advocated the employment of little children in the mills—mills "whose establishment he was urging should be by a protective tariff."

It was feared at the time that the labor supply for agriculture would be put in danger by creating a demand for workers in manufacturing. But Hamilton—Abbott informs us—offered an answer: "Adult men," he said in his famous *Report on Manufactures* [1791], "were not needed in a machine equipped factory; women and children of eight and ten 'who would otherwise be idle' could be used as operators in the textile mills."

And so it happened:

> The machinery which came from England for what was then truly an infant [young] industry, was especially built to accommodate little children. The regulation of child labor in this country was delayed [Abbott held] not because the leaders in social reform were converted to the ruthless industrial patriotism of Hamilton, but because of the absorbing struggle over the abolition of slavery and the problems of reconstruction [that] followed the Civil War . . . The real child labor movement did not get underway until the last decade of the nineteenth century.

Grace resigned her position as head of the Children's Bureau in 1934 in order to join her sister's faculty at Chicago as professor of Public Welfare, feeling that Perkins would defend the bureau from forces allied against it. However as the Social Security Act reached its final stage, the Children's Bureau's largest responsibility—aid to dependent children—was placed under the administration of the new

Social Security Board. This loss to the bureau marked the beginning of the dismemberment of its "whole-child policy" embodied in a single department.

While the loss was a major one, funds nevertheless were allotted for programs designed by the bureau, so that Grace could remain positive about the future, writing in her 1938 book *The Child and the State*:

> The cause of children must always triumph ultimately. The important thing is that we should be "on our way" toward adequately meeting their needs. Perhaps you may ask, "Does the road lead uphill all the way?" And I must answer, "Yes, to the very end." But if I offer you a long, hard struggle, I can also promise you great rewards. Justice for all children is the high ideal in a democracy. It is the special responsibility of women. We have hardly, as yet, been able to make more than a beginning in the realization of that great objective.

(A reorganization of the Children's Bureau in 1946 made function, not constituency, the decisive factor. This change in the name of "efficiency" resulted in the bureau being transferred to the new Federal Security Agency—and in 1953 to the Department of Health, Education, and Welfare "as a shadow of its former self.")

No longer a government administrator, Grace threw herself in succeeding years into a busy schedule of teaching, writing, and meetings—including two conferences of the International Labor Organization in Geneva, Switzerland, and a Pan-American Child Congress in Mexico. Back in 1923, she had been the first person sent to represent the United States at the League of Nations, on a committee investigating worldwide "Traffic in Women and Children."

Perkins offered her one of the three Social Security Board positions for implementing the Social Security Act in 1935. Although favorably disposed to accepting the challenge, she declined for health reasons, having experienced two difficult bouts of tuberculosis—one in 1928 of nine months and a second in 1931–1932 of almost a year, both spent recovering at a high altitude in Colorado.

Then, in 1938, she learned that she had an incurable form of cancer. Her death in 1939 at age sixty left her sister Edith grief-stricken, and was reported in newspapers throughout the country. It evoked letters and telegrams from supporters in "all walks of life," moved by her years of working for women and children. In a special tribute, Harvard law professor Felix Frankfurter praised her "rare art of public administration," calling "the manner in which she translated the blueprints of social policies into effective operating institutions for the benefit of society, work in every true sense of the phrase, that of social invention."

She managed to keep her spirits up almost to the end, except for a nagging concern about war:

> One thinks of the European situation constantly [she wrote to her niece Charlotte]; it forms an ominous background to everything.

Her final, posthumous work, *From Relief to Social Security*, spoke of: "perhaps the most important factor in all our child welfare problems . . . the regular employment of the father at a reasonable wage" [using the traditional family model]. In her words:

> Normal unemployment with recurring depressions of greater or less degree constitute for the worker and his family one of the most serious hazards of our industrial system. This type of unemployment is due in part to the fact that industry counts on a reserve labor supply to meet its peak seasonal demands and has in the past dismissed its workers without notice when demand fell off, with no responsibility to them or to the community for their maintenance until they were again needed . . .
>
> With stabilization accomplished, change comes again [she stated], suddenly and disastrously for many

individuals . . . Unemployment, therefore, may be regarded in greater or less degree as the inevitable result of our industrial system. A democracy which supports this system should, therefore, make adequate and democratic provision for its victims . . .

———³ ᵇ———

Meanwhile Edith had recognized early-on that expanding welfare during the Depression—and subsequently in New Deal relief programs—would require competent social welfare administrators. She resolved to meet that need without sacrificing educational standards, and assumed a personal role in placing her graduate students in key public positions. With the same conviction she'd felt towards gaining woman's suffrage, she now sought to achieve a "safety net" for all Americans through a comprehensive system of social security.

The Federal Emergency Relief Administration (FERA), introduced during the first year of the Roosevelt administration, received her "qualified approval." Its administrator Harry Hopkins had been a social worker in a New York settlement, he'd risen through the ranks, and he stood for the fundamental principles of the field. But she "could not accept the justice of the federal government's ending 'this business of relief' in two years—before the assistance programs of the Social Security Act were ready to function, and before any permanent, modern public welfare substitute could be put in place."

(As it transpired, an extension of emergency relief—the Work Projects Administration [WPA]—succeeded FERA, with a public works program directed by Hopkins replacing "the dole." Until the economy recovered due to wartime production, the WPA built up infrastructure and provided community, cultural, and conservation projects for the unemployed.)

To the regret of both Abbott sisters, health insurance and long-term unemployment remained unaddressed in the 1935 Social Security Act—the former drawing such fierce resistance from the American Medical Association that it put the entire legislation in jeopardy. It was difficult, too, for Edith to reconcile herself to a "means test" as a basis for social welfare policy. Instead, she cited the example of free instruction supplemented by free books in education, "not for poor children alone but for all children."

Sixteen years later at age seventy-five—upon being honored by the National Conference of Social Work—she delivered a strongly-felt statement on the same subject:

> I want to take my last minute for what I consider the most important next step for us to take in social work, and that is to get rid of the "means test" . . . for example, by [providing] a benefit for all children . . . and by [extending] Old Age pensions to everyone at a certain age . . .
>
> Social Security is still not social security [she added] if we give only to those who can prove that they are destitute . . . This is one of the new Roads to Freedom that we need a little courage to find.

# Journey's End

The three early giants of Hull-House—Addams, Lathrop, and Kelley—did not live to see the New Deal enact social legislation they'd struggled so hard to realize. Kelley and Lathrop died within months of each other, in February and April 1932. Kelley had found no letup in the twenties. The Child Labor Amendment failed to gain approval, and a split arose in the women's movement between professionals who advocated an equal rights amendment, and reformers who'd fought for protective legislation. (Not until 1970 in a milestone case would a US Court of Appeals rule that jobs need to be "substantially equal" but not "identical" to fall under the protection of the 1963 Equal Pay Act.)

For some two decades, though, Kelley did manage to spend time in the summer at her farmhouse retreat on the Maine coast, returning to New York refreshed and invigorated each fall.

During the twenties, Lathrop served as assessor of the League of Nations' Child Welfare Commission, advisor to the National Child Labor Committee, and president of the Illinois League of Women Voters. The final months of her life were "filled with concern over the impending execution of a young criminal from Rockford, who was still a minor . . ." Her opposition to capital punishment—and specifically her appeal against the execution of minors—grew into a nation-wide cause. The trial became "one of the most widely publicized of a juvenile in the United States . . ." A year and a half later, the case ended with a new Illinois governor commuting the sentence from death to lifetime imprisonment.

In April 1935, Addams traveled to Washington, as an honored guest at the twentieth-anniversary celebration of the founding of the Women's International League for Peace and Freedom. Twelve hundred attended, including the President's wife Eleanor Roosevelt, a former settlement house volunteer and one of the principle speakers (who would eventually serve as United States delegate to the new United Nations.)

The next month, Addams learned that she had cancer in an advanced stage. Her death soon after at age seventy-four was mourned world-wide. At Hull-House "thousands passed by her coffin, and hundreds attended the memorial service in the courtyard." The burial took place in the village cemetery of Cedarville, her birthplace.

Edith Abbott and Alice Hamilton—the last of the "six remarkable Hull-House women"—reached the ages of eighty-one and one-hundred-and-one respectively, in 1957 and 1970. Edith went back to her family home in Grand Island, Nebraska, in her final years, where she found life much changed from the heady days of her youth.

Hamilton, who retired from Harvard in 1935, acted as a medical advisor on labor standards during the New Deal. After World War II, she grew disillusioned with the country's foreign policy—its preoccupation with communism abroad, leading to the infringement of personal liberties at home. The end of her life was spent with her sister Margaret at their house in Hadlyme, Connecticut, which overlooked the Connecticut River.

By the 1920s, Hull-House activities offered a range of "fully developed programs" with a staff of experienced leaders, many of whom were longtime residents—for example, the directors of the Music and Art schools, Theater, and the Juvenile Protective Association. During its years of expansion, the settlement provided opportunities to thousands of neighbors weekly, mainly second-generation and often highly motivated immigrants.

In the period following Addams' death, Hull-House underwent considerable upheaval and change, as did its Near West Side neighborhood, which in 1963 became the site of a Chicago campus of the University of Illinois. Only the original Hull mansion survived, reconstructed at the new university as a museum, archives, and conference center. As a social service organization, Hull-House operated with associate agencies in the city to provide child care, education, job training, housing assistance, and a program to counter domestic violence.

Then in January 2012, due to unsustainable debt and a crisis in funding during recession, the settlement abruptly closed—more than a hundred and twenty years after its founding.

## Sources

Abbott, Edith. *Truancy and Non-Attendance in the Chicago Schools.* New York: Arno Press, 1970, 353.

Abbott, Grace. *From Relief to Social Security.* NY: Russell & Russell, 1966, 4–5.

———. *Grace Abbott Reader.* John Sorensen, ed., with Judith Sealander. Lincoln: University of Nebraska Press, 2008, 72–73, 80.

Addams, Jane. *My Friend, Julia Lathrop.* Urbana: University of Illinois Press, 2004, 150–153.

Bryan, Mary Lynn McCree, and Allen F. Davis, eds. *100 Years at Hull-House.* Bloomington: Indiana University Press, 1990, 207-285.

Commager, Henry Steele. *Growth of the American Republic,* vol. 2. New York: Oxford University Press, 1980, chapter XX.

Costin, Lela. *Two Sisters for Social Justice.* Urbana: University of Illinois Press, 1983, 90–94, chapters 9–10.

Downey, Kirstin. *The Woman Behind the New Deal: the Life of Frances Perkins.* New York: Doubleday, 2009, 33–37, 230–246.

Fitzpatrick, Ellen. *Endless Crusade.* New York: Oxford University Press, 1990, 211–212, 216.

Golay, Michael. *America 1933*. New York: Free Press, 2013, 119–147.

Kirkland, Wallace. *The Many Faces of Hull-House: Photographs of Wallace Kirkland*. Edited by Mary Ann Johnson. Urbana: University of Illinois Press, 1989, pp.7, 18–19, 27, 30–31, 33, 35.

Lindenmeyer, Kriste. *"A Right to Childhood": The U.S. Children's Bureau and Child Welfare, 1912–46*. Urbana: University of Illinois Press, 1997, 249–261.

Muncy, Robyn. *Creating a Female Dominion in American Reform*. NY: Oxford University Press, 1991, 153–157.

Perkins, Frances. *The Roosevelt I Knew*. New York: Viking Press, 1946, 257.

*Schultz v. Wheaton Glass Co.* 1970 U.S. Court of Appeals for the Third Circuit. Internet: Infoplease.com.

Thayer, Kate. "Hull-House closing Friday." *Chicago Tribune*, January 25, 2012.

# Index

# Credits for Photographs

**HULL-HOUSE SETTLEMENT PICTURES** used with permission of the University of Illinois at Chicago Library, Department of Special Collections

**Bowen Country Club photographs**, Wallace Kirkland photographer:

>*Boy sketching,* #38. JAMC_0420_1174
>*Boy smelling flowers,* #51. JAMC_0406_4700
>*Dance tableau,* #166. JAMC_0414_4792
>*Girl with pinwheel,* #213. JAMC_0402_4584
>*Swing,* #407. JAMC_0402_4590

**Hull-House Yearbook collection:**

>*Violin lesson,* #24. JAMC_0000_0184_1121
>*At a Hull-House recital,* #27. HHYB_1927_023
>*Hull-House boys band,* #64. JAMC_0000_0113_2491
>*In the pottery class,* #89. JAMC_0000_0299_1036

**Seven Settlements collection - Hull-House series:**

>*Girl glazing pottery,* #410. JAMC_0000_0066_0604
>*Kindergartners with teacher,* #415. JAMC_0000_0095_0109a
>*Five teen actors striking poses,* #485. JAMC_0000_0350_4103
>*Former Hull-House boy Benny Goodman playing clarinet for*
>    *settlement children,* #496. JAMC_0000_0443_5719

**THE LEWIS HINE CHILD LABOR PICTURES** used courtesy of the Library of Congress, Prints & Photographs Division

**National Child Labor Committee Collection:**

>*A little spinner,* digital ID: nclc 05395
>*Five-year-old "newsie,"* digital ID: nclc 05320
>*Nine-year-old tobacco picker,* digital ID: cph 3a01112
>*"Dinner-toter,"* digital ID: nclc 05343